My dearest Toyin

Thank you for being a part
of my life. You bring joy +
sunshine to us. I pray
God's blessings and His showers
of love in your life. May God's
grace continue to shine in your
life.

Enjoy "Footprints of Grace" +
wish you many more of
God's richness & faithfulness
to flourish in life.

Lots of love

Busola Sodinde

08·09·17

FOOTPRINTS OF GRACE

REDISCOVERING SELF IN CHRIST

DAVINA HART

Footprints of Grace
Rediscovering Self in Christ

We want to hear from you. Please send your comments about this book to us at:
Publisher FOG Series
Email: FOG@fogseries.com
Website: www.fogseries.com

British Library Cataloguing in Publication Data
A catalogue record for this book is available from the British Library

ISBN – 978-1-9998433-0-4

Printed and bound in Great Britain
Requests for information should be addressed to:
FOG Series, International House, 142 Cromwell Road, Kensington, London, SW7 4EF

Table of Contents

Dedication

This is dedicated to the next generation so that they know that the promises they see today are because of God's continuous faithfulness to us. God performs 'Red Sea' miracles in our lives to exhibit His greatness and reaffirm His love as a Father. Our Faith in Christ is the inheritance we want to leave for the next generation.

God is El-Shaddai. This name means "God Almighty, "the God who is all-sufficient and all-bountiful, the source of all blessings".

Introduction

A bit about the writer

I'm not a writer by profession. I currently work in Financial Services in the City of London and will be turning 40 at the time of writing this book. I was born into a Christian family and have been a Christian all my life. Even though I became born-again in my early twenties, I only realised two years ago, that there was a lot that was made available to me than I drew out of my faith.

What happened to me for 20-odd years after becoming a born-again Christian? Why hadn't I fully lived the life that God chose for me? Why did I only scratch at the surface? What had changed?

I was busy, distracted and battling tough decisions on my own for most of the time and as time went on, daily challenges became much tougher. I got to a crossroad where I had exhausted all means and in August 2015, I cried to God to reveal more of Himself to me; to re-emphasise, I was a Christian but I knew that I wasn't living a tenth of how the Bible described life to be lived.

What happened to me next prompted me to write this book. I had a total transformation and renewal of my mind and it has been a revelation journey since then. I now talk to God every day and I use the access Jesus gave us to grow in my relationship of knowing God intimately. This intimacy with Christ has transformed me and underpins everything that brings me joy.

People often ask when they meet someone new what their interests are. I get asked,"What are you most passionate about?". In the past, I would have said that I love cooking, listening to music, participating in sport and travelling. I still enjoy these things but I have realised that I have a much deeper passion; my interests are embedded in my passion for Christ. I love activities that draw me close to God and what I cherish is spending time with people and sharing the joy and stories of our dependence on God. This is what gives me the most joy. Loving God and loving others.

This book is for anyone who can identify with stories and moments in my life. I want to tell them that God is real and we have more at our disposal if we continue to grow in our intimacy with Christ. What do I mean by this statement? I have experienced several miracles over the years as a Christian but it is easy for us to think that because we see miracles happen in our lives, that our relationship with Christ is mature.

This is not true. In fact, miracles only remind us that Jesus is Lord to increase our level of faith and draw us to God. Intimacy in Christ extends our relationship with Him, it goes beyond

INTRODUCTION

miracles. It's a place of constant joy, deep peace and exponential love.

There are many books detailing personal encounters of God and we may think that our individual stories are personal, should not be shared, are irrelevant to a wider audience, or even mind blowing but we don't feel confident in letting it out that we are Christians. The good news is that our intimacy with God transforms us, we are able to connect with Him through our spirit, and He gives us the boldness we need, to tell others about Him.

God uses ordinary people; the least qualified, to show the deep power of the Holy Spirit. This book explores the journey of intimacy with God and a desire to leave behind our footprints in Christ.

Joshua 4: 21 - 24

21   "Then Joshua said to the Israelites, "In the future your children will ask, 'what do these stones mean?'

22   Then you can tell them, 'This is where the Israelites crossed the Jordan on dry ground.'

23   For the Lord your God dried up the river right before your eyes, and he kept it dry until you were all across, just as he did at the Red Sea when he dried it up until we had all crossed over.

24   He did this so all the nations of the earth might know that the Lord's hand is powerful, and so you might fear the Lord your God forever."

The diagram below illustrates my roadmap, my thoughts, which the personal stories in this book highlight

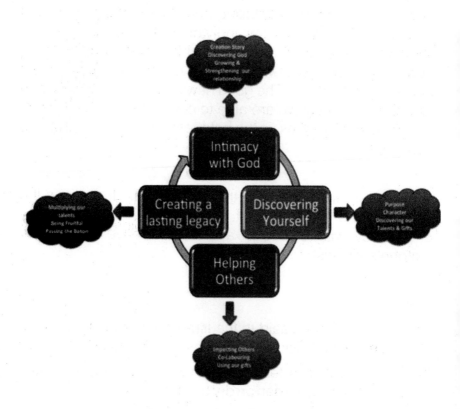

Part I

Chapter 1

In The Beginning

I was born into a Christian family and always accepted my faith in God. This faith went unchallenged for years as I have always ticked the questionnaire boxes when asked what my religion was. I did this very naturally without questioning what Christianity really meant.

Later in life, I was faced with the opportunity to address the things I took for granted. I woke up in my twenties and became more conscious of the big decisions I was having to make, where I would live, what my career options were, what type of man I would marry; and also, what faith really meant?

I wanted to know how my faith in God will help me make the right life changing decisions and more importantly, I asked, "What is the meaning of life and why am I here?" These questions took me on a journey to explore my faith in Christ and it started with me picking up the Bible again.

I began by reading from the book of Genesis, the first chapter. On this occasion, I immersed myself and reflected on what I read. In the past, I had read the book without understanding the significance of why God created the world. I read it again and this time, I also read other commentaries that other authors had written about this topic.

The creation story is a beautiful story, which ended too soon, as I got reading, it dawned on me that God created man for a relationship. He created mankind in His image and likeness.

Genesis 1: 27-28

27.   "So God created mankind in his own image, in the image of God he created them; male and female he created them.

28.   God blessed them and said to them, "Be fruitful and increase in number; fill the earth and subdue it."

Adam was given the responsibility to take care of the garden and look after the animals and plants. He was given dominion over all things but was instructed however, not to eat from the tree of the knowledge of good and evil.

Genesis 2: 8-9, 15-17

8.   "Then the Lord God planted a garden in Eden in the east, and there he placed the man he had made.

9.   The Lord God made all sorts of trees grow up from the ground—trees that were beautiful and that produced delicious fruit. In the middle of the garden he placed the tree of life and the tree of the knowledge of good and evil.

15. The Lord God placed the man in the Garden of Eden to tend and watch over it.

16. But the Lord God warned him, "You may freely eat the fruit of every tree in the garden—

17. Except the tree of the knowledge of good and evil. If you eat its fruit, you are sure to die"

As I turned the pages, into chapter three, I saw that man's relationship with God was broken through sin. We see that Eve was tempted by the serpent in the garden and ate the forbidden fruit. She also gave Adam the apple, which he took and ate, but they had to leave the Garden of Eden as a consequence of their sins.

Genesis 3: 22-23

22. "And the Lord God said, "The man has now become like one of us, knowing good and evil. He must not be allowed to reach out his hand and take also from the tree of life and eat, and live forever."

23. So the Lord God banished him from the Garden of Eden to work the ground from which he had been taken."

After reading the creation story, I reckoned that if the first sin hadn't occurred, we would still be in constant fellowship with God; enjoying all that He created as He intended from the beginning. I reflected on this and pondered on why God created the tree of conscience. Why was this tree put in the beautiful Garden of Eden? Why didn't God put a physical barrier to stop man from eating the forbidden fruit? Why didn't

God stop Eve? It must have been the most painful experience to watch when Adam and Eve let sin in.

I recently watched the creation story with my children so that they would learn about how the world was created and the events that took place in the Garden of Eden. I remember their eyes fixed on the television and watching the moment Eve ate the fruit from the forbidden tree, the look on their faces was that of shock. They had their faces covered with both hands like they were watching a horror movie. For the first time, I had a glimpse of how God must have felt in that moment.

God loves us so much that He gave us the gift of free will. Would it have been better if God controlled us so that we won't make mistakes, take responsibility for our actions, have no sin and live in the Garden of Eden for life? I pondered on this thought. I am quite a rational, logical person and I have found that when I ask these questions, God uses very simple illustrations to explain.

Whether we are conscious of it or not, we have been formed with the desire to be free. In other words, we are not to be controlled by anyone or force, but for our actions to be driven out of love. This is consistent with humanity, whether we believe in God or not; we are not wired to be controlled beings. When we think we are being controlled, we act in a rebellious manner to break that feeling; no one likes being restrained.

We feel completely free when love operates at its best. God created the world and formed man in His image and because

IN THE BEGINNING

He is love, we were formed out of love. God gave us free will so that we can choose to have a relationship with Him. For we know that anything we choose out of our freewill is where genuine love resides. This is the same choice that God has given to us; to choose to follow Him each day.

Back to the story, the tree was placed right in the middle of the garden; poking our subconscious to choose to love God by trusting Him on His Word. He gave His blessings for man to have all things but not eat the fruit of the tree of knowledge of good and evil; the forbidden fruit.

The same motive to know everything, was and still is man's desire to discern as God does. Man's first sin is ever present in our lives, however, when we choose to live our lives guided by the Word of God and submit to God's ways, we reciprocate His love and the Lord blesses our obedience.

My faith in Christ grew as I learnt more about God. The more I understood His love and grace, the more I wanted to be in God's presence; the Garden of Eden. This changed my perspective on how I viewed my life. I started building my relationship with God when I understood why I was created. I now enjoy God's daily provisions and have conversations with Him everyday.

I am thankful that the story didn't end with man becoming disconnected from God but He restored us all back again through His son, Jesus Christ. God loved us so much that He sent His only son, Jesus Christ, to show us how to live and by accepting Jesus Christ as our Saviour, we can restore this relationship and transform our lives. Jesus separates us from our sin so that we can have intimacy with God.

John 3:16-17

16.   "For this is how God loved the world: He gave his one and only Son, so that everyone who believes in him will not perish but have eternal life.

17.   God sent his Son into the world not to judge the world, but to save the world through him."

Going back to the questions I had about how to deal with life's decisions, it became easier when I realised that I could have a conversation with God; I didn't feel alone anymore. In fact, I had the opposite feeling, I felt that God expected me to talk to Him about it and trust Him. My faith and obedience pleased God. I may not know all the answers, in spite of this, when I put my trust in the Lord, God was delighted and my relationship was formed. Our faith in Christ is a key component to an intimate relationship with God.

Hebrews 11:1-3

"Faith shows the reality of what we hope for; it is the evidence of things we cannot see. Through their faith, the people in days of old earned a good reputation. By faith we understand that the entire universe was formed at God's command, that what we now see did not come from anything that can be seen."

Over the years, I have had what seemed like very challenging requests and some simple requests answered in ways I would never have imagined. Each time my prayers were answered, I felt more reassured of His presence and it sealed my relationship completely. God was no longer an abstract being but He became a real person who communicates with us.

We have the same access as was intended from the beginning; to know God intimately through Christ. He carries us to a place of authentic worship and builds us up to depend on God for all our needs by trusting Him.

Hebrews 8:11

"No longer will they teach their neighbour, or say to one another, 'Know the Lord,' because they will all know me, from the least of them to the greatest."

I now love starting my day with God by talking to Him. I tell Him how I'm feeling, how I expect my day to be and that He should always be with me. This is my daily prayer, to be continuously conscious of the presence of God and live every moment in 'our' relationship.

Points for Reflection

We need to imagine how God intended for us to live in the 'Garden of Eden'.

The book of Proverbs 8:30-31says,

30.   "Then I was constantly at his side. I was filled with delight day after day, rejoicing always in his presence,

31.   Rejoicing in his whole world and delighting in mankind..."

God wants us to consciously live in His presence enjoying all that He created for us. The flowers, the sun, the moon and bright stars, water, rain, the wind, the birds, the plants, the fish in the sea, the land animals, relationships, and intimacy between husband and wife, desiring one another and procreating.

These gifts are free and designed to give us the pleasures of a good life. There's a saying "the best things in life are free", and Christ gave freely of Himself, by dying for us so we can have an abundant life through our faith in Him. When we enjoy God's provision and delight ourselves in Him, God draws us close to Himself with an assurance of who we are in Him. He loves us despite our weaknesses.

Romans 5: 6-8

6.   "You see, at just the right time, when we were still powerless, Christ died for the ungodly.

7.   Very rarely will anyone die for a righteous person, though for a good person someone might possibly dare to die.

8.   But God demonstrates his own love for us in this: While we were still sinners, Christ died for us."

IN THE BEGINNING

1 John 4:19

"We love because He first loved us."

Proverbs 8:17

"I love them that love me; and those that seek me diligently shall find me."

Ephesians 6:24

"Grace be with all them that love our Lord Jesus Christ with a love incorruptible."

Discovering God

"You will seek me and find me when you seek me with all your heart."

Jeremiah 29:13

I wish I had made the decision earlier to know God and have a better appreciation of why I was created. Reading the Bible is an obvious place to start, but unfortunately, I didn't make it a priority; instead, I followed other paths that I thought made me happy. I followed the crowd without a sense of purpose until I experienced my personal dilemmas and searched for the truth.

On a practical side, I am quite culpable because I often don't read manuals when I buy most electrical items, gadget or smart phone. I simply don't bother because I expect them to function or receive and make phone calls as expected.

However, I can sincerely say that the phone only functions at its basic level because I haven't applied all the settings for it to work as a high-tech gadget – which was the reason why I paid a fortune for it. I use the manual only when there's a basic malfunction and I'm panicking.

Such similarities exist in our faith; where we are blindly unaware of our access to God who helps us to live beyond just getting by. We need to know that we were created to have access to a constant guardian who watches over us. We are equipped to deal with life with the tools God has blessed us with, which are accessible through a relationship with Christ, as Christ has paid a high price for our salvation.

We invest our time obtaining a good education and trying to be good citizens. We feel very proud when we succeed at school and graduate with good jobs. I had these feelings too. As a child, I didn't give my parents much hassle and did well in school. However, I soon realised that what I learnt couldn't address my unanswered questions, especially, when I felt lost. I asked my parents the obvious questions and they did all they could to explain what they knew.

There were also times when I couldn't articulate when something was wrong. In those moments, I pressed the panic button and secretly spoke to an unknown unfamiliar God and looking back, in His kindness, God looked after me. There is something mysterious about a child knowing good and evil even when not taught about it.

IN THE BEGINNING

Growing up, I attended Sunday school and our teachers read lovely stories from the Bible to us – David and Goliath, Noah's Ark, Joseph with the coat of many colours, Daniel in the lion's den. However, we were told these stories as you would a fairy tale, which is a great style to engage little ones but it doesn't necessarily equip them.

Our coping mechanisms as children often appear to be self-taught, but I'd say God watches over us and those moments draw us to God. A child soon discovers that there is something out there greater than the protection that an earthly parent can give. I learnt this quickly especially at bed times or after a scary dream, where I was often encouraged to sleep tight and pray. I was told that there were angels guarding us. I learnt how to judge new situations and I had conversations with this unfamiliar person.

I remember distinctively, my earliest childhood memory of feeling slightly apprehensive when I was five years old. I remember being frightened when we moved to another country and attended a new school. I remember crying and my father explained to the teacher that we had just moved and he requested she help settle me into the new environment. I sat next to the teacher for a few weeks until I became comfortable in my new class. My father's love for me was reassuring; he was there most times, looking out for me. He showered me with love and attention.

Growing up, I had a happy life being the middle child. In some ways, the 'middle-child' syndrome of being overlooked can be true but I became quite independent, as I didn't have people fussing over me.

I felt quite confident and asked to go to boarding school, without fully grasping that I was going to be away from my family for long periods of time. After a term and realising that it wasn't that much fun, I pleaded with my father to change my school but he ignored my pleas, and for reasons best known to him, he kept me there. In hindsight, that built my resilience. My father, however never left me; he visited almost every other week, which was quite uncommon. I knew it broke his heart seeing me unhappy but he made sure I felt very loved.

I moved back to England at the age of seventeen to continue my education and came to study without my family. I was alone and this time, there were no accompanying weekly visits. I felt very lonely and scared. During my difficult times, I retreated into my secret place to access my unseen guiding angel. I started asking questions about God, asked for help and looking back now, the Lord was revealing Himself to me as Father. He provided for me, kept me out of trouble and became my shelter.

I became more confident and as time passed by, I had discovered a new relationship with my Father in Heaven who was and is far greater than my earthly father. My earthly father's love was solid but it was God's hand that kept me all the time. Each time He saw me distressed as a child and when I called on Him, He answered by protecting me. He made sure my earthly father embraced me just at the right time.

When we invite Him in and ask for help, He takes the front seat; the steering wheel and changes our path to His.

We may or may not have a story of a person who played a significant role in our lives; however, I am confident that the absolute love of the Father is present to those who call and know him as Abba Father. It is comforting to know that God is near and we don't have to look far to find Him. God is our ever-present help in time of need.

Psalm 46:1

"God is our refuge and strength, an ever-present help in trouble."

Acts 2:21

"But everyone who calls on the name of the Lord will be saved."

Developing an Intimate Relationship with God

"Search and Discovery is a Journey not a Destination"

Discovering God is the best investment a person can make but it doesn't stop there. Discovering God is a start but we need to continue talking to God not just in critical times of our lives but all the time. To develop our relationship further, we need to communicate frequently, to create an intimate bond between God and us. John 8:31 says, "If you continue in my word, you are truly my disciples."

As I developed my relationship with God, I found myself actively seeking to know my purpose. I struggled with this, as I had prioritised the desire to know my purpose before a hunger for a deeper relationship with God. I wanted to act out my love without investing in knowing God more

Bill Johnson in his book, Hosting the Presence, expressed the intimacy that we can have when we discover God's ways. He mentions further that God longs for us to communicate with Him and tell Him what is in our hearts. This invitation in the relationship allows us to experience who God is.

We can miss the intimacy of our relationships if we assumed our roles without understanding how to connect with the people in those relationships. You can be a father who works hard all day to pay the bills but you can also be a father who first understands his family's needs and priorities and consciously alters his hours to enhance the quality of life at home.

We need to know God's heart to create a more harmonious outcome. God is interested in all aspects of our lives and it is to our benefit that we should also seek to know His heart.

Intimacy with God also ensures that we are not burnt out from life's worries as we rely on God first. Without it, we deny ourselves the restoration that is needed in our lives daily. I have learnt the importance of intimacy in periods of uncertainty over my twenty years of being a Christian. In these periods, the grace of God removes our insecurities. God's love is perfect and it casts out all fears.

1John 4:18

"There is no fear in love; but perfect love casts out fear, because fear involves torment. But he who fears has not been made perfect in love."

Let me explain with the story of Job in the Bible. Job was an upright man, blameless and described as a man of complete integrity. However, Satan says that it is because of the grace of God that Job sought God and asked for God's protection to be removed for a period. The book of Job gives a detailed account of when Job is attacked by Satan; he lost his family and livelihood and became very dejected.

Towards the end of his torment, he deliberated about why these things happened to him and used a list of good deeds and services as his defence. He thought those would protect him from harm. Consequently, he questioned God and there was an interesting exchange of words.

When we start a relationship without the desire to pursue intimacy as our core foundation, we would struggle later when issues arise. We make the mistake of co-existing in such relationships and assume our roles too quickly without finding out more about the other person. Inevitably, we end up feeling quite bewildered if we don't understand our partner's actions.

Job misunderstood what was expected in his relationship with God and here we can read his response. Job says,"...now I was talking about things I knew nothing about..." (Job 42:3).

Job 42: 1-6

1.   "Then Job replied to the Lord:

2.   I know that you can do anything, and no one can stop you.

3.   You asked, 'Who is this that questions my wisdom with such ignorance?'It is I—and I was talking about things I knew nothing about, things far too wonderful for me.

4.   You said, 'Listen and I will speak! I have some questions for you, and you must answer them.'

5.   I had only heard about you before, but now I have seen you with my own eyes.

6.   I take back everything I said, and I sit in dust and ashes to show my repentance."

Some Christians go to church to sit and listen to sermons about God but they haven't invested the time to know Him intimately. It is vitally important that we develop a personal relationship with God, know His nature, His ways and what pleases Him, so that we can enjoy the full extent of the relationship that has been made available to us.

Points for Reflection

·   God wants us to develop a deep level of intimacy with Him.

- God wants us to come to Him daily for our bread (the bread of life).
- God wants us to call Him Abba Father.

Galatians 2:16

"Yet we know that a person is made right with God by faith in Jesus Christ, not by obeying the law. And we have believed in Christ Jesus, so that we might be made right with God because of our faith in Christ, not because we have obeyed the law. For no one will ever be made right with God by obeying the law."

Prayer of Certainty in God

Dear Lord,

You opened the heavens and asked us for our containers to receive Your blessings. My container is my heart, because in You I have everything.

You are my heart's desire, as You intended from the beginning. I pray that You fill me up to worship You in spirit and in truth.

Jesus - You came to open the door, that anyone who believes in You will have eternal life, so that we do not die but spend eternity in heaven, being with our Creator and joining all creation to worship our Father.

You said not to care about tomorrow and not to worry; the key to life is in Your hands.

So here I am Lord, waiting for You, to mould me, to shape me, to strengthen me, to build me up, to build my faith, to establish me right in your presence.

I live my life to be holy and consecrated to You, to love and worship You.

Amen.

Chapter 2

Intimacy with God

Growing in Love

"So often we become so focused on the finish line that we fail to enjoy the journey."

- Deiter F Uchtdorf

Our relationship with God is an eternal one; we start here to finish in Heaven. Growing in love involves building a strong relationship so that we can develop deep roots to give us a firm foundation. Our love for God needs time to grow and spending lots of alone-time with God helps – He reveals His person to us.

Paul likens our Christian journey to that of an endurance test, telling us to run with perseverance. It is a long road ahead often with bumps and tight corners and we may crash if we find ourselves running too fast in the first few miles. Paul urges us to invest in our love for Christ and to grow in faith by spending time with God.

2 Timothy 1: 13

"Hold tightly to the pattern of truth I taught you, especially concerning the faith and love Christ Jesus offers you."

We can also understand how we can grow spiritually by relating this to a newborn baby. Peter says, like newborn babies, crave pure spiritual milk, so that by it you may grow up in your salvation (1 Peter 2:2). During a baby's growth spurt, he or she will feed and sleep up to 20 hours a day and over time, the baby learns to crawl, then walk, stand on its feet and eventually run.

On the contrary, the world around us pumps information into our subconscious that we must run faster than our legs can carry us, therefore, we feel the pressure to perform. These simple truths to slow down are too often ignored and it's no wonder we see individuals burn out when the pressure takes its toll on them. Paul says we can suddenly find ourselves striving rather than depending on God in these situations.

2 Corinthians 1: 8-9

8.   "We were under great pressure, far beyond our ability to endure, so that we despaired of life itself.

9.   Indeed, we felt we had received the sentence of death. But this happened that we might not rely on ourselves but on God, who raises the dead".

I have some good news to share, if we are feeling under pressure to perform in any way, Jesus says to come as we are.

Matthew 11:28

"Come to me and I will give you rest—all of you who work so hard beneath a heavy yoke. Wear my yoke—for it fits perfectly—and let me teach you; for I am gentle and humble, and you shall find rest for your souls; for I give you only light burdens."

The best gift of any relationship is when we allow ourselves and those we choose to be with, to feel secure in who they are. God does not require us to run as fast as we can, imagine or over perform, instead, God tells us to come to a place of rest. In our rest, we enjoy the beauty of true intimacy.

He loves our dependence on Him so that we do not rely solely on our abilities but we allow God in the decision-making process.

John 15.5

He who abides in Me, and I in him, bears much fruit; for without Me you can do nothing

Our busyness and over-working breeds distractions, which can create more distance in our relationships. When we pause and take time out to remember Him who created all things – all things, including human beings, it glorifies God.

Genesis 2:1-3

1.   "So the creation of the heavens and the earth and everything in them was completed.

2.   On the seventh day God had finished his work of
      creation, so he rested from all his work.

3.   And God blessed the seventh day and declared it holy,
      because it was the day when he rested from all his work
      of creation."

The prophet Isaiah in Isaiah 58:13 stated that this special time
of rest means:

-    To enjoy the presence of God and delight in His
     presence

-    Honouring Him with our time

-    Worshipping God

We can understand better how to live and grow in our
relationship with God by looking at the life of Jesus:

·   Jesus relied on His relationship with God, His Father,
     such that he periodically withdrew from people and the
     heavy demands of His ministry to be alone with God.

·   Jesus sought out a quiet place to rest and fellowship
     with God.

·   Jesus' solitude led to a deeper relationship with the
     God He knew as Abba.

I read an article on soul sheperding[1] about Jesus' solitude and
silence and it raised an important question - How could we
think that we can live well without following Jesus' example?
Spending time with Jesus should be our first assignment.

Accepting rest (sabbath) should no longer be a command but an attitude of the heart to devote time for being in God's presence and worshipping Him.

Jesus declared"For the Son of Man is Lord even of the Sabbath" (Matthew 12:8).

My resting times have drawn me closer into God's presence and He refreshes my soul daily. The best part of my day is my bed time because after a long day, I finally get to settle down, relax, unwind and tell God about my day. It has become a necessary self-imposed discipline.

An article from Health.com stated that "Researchers at Harvard University and Boston College found that people seem to strengthen the emotional components of memory during sleep" and I have to agree with this. The more assured I was in Christ, the more I became very dependent on Him and craved more intimacy, I resisted the need to over-perform.

I found that trying to balance our time with God and daily commitments can be a bit challenging when we first start to cultivate this habit. It is not an easy routine; we wrestle at first because it's totally contrary to how people live with various competing priorities. In those moments, we shouldn't feel stressed as Jesus tells us to come as we are. A short pause during the day to read a Bible verse and think about God, gets us going. We eventually become more disciplined and better at it with time, as we increase our daily devotion and grow in our faith.

Spending time with Jesus is essential to growing physically, emotionally and spiritually. Newborn babies need plenty of rest to grow; we need plenty of rest to repair our cells; perform at our best at work and we need plenty of rest in Jesus to replenish our soul.

Whenever I find myself feeling stressed when juggling daily tasks and distractions, I deliberately take time out to read my Bible and pray, it helps to reset my priorities. I pray for fewer distractions and that the fear of missing out will disappear.

One of the ways I have developed my quality time with God is by waking up early before my children do - the house is quieter at such times and I can have my alone time with God.

My husband and I also wanted to impart these values to our children and so we decided as a family to stop everything once a week for a few hours, to fellowship together, eat together, sing hymns and share the word of God. My children love it because we have also exemplified this special bond with God to them.

They see us cancelling social invitations and putting our phones away during our family time. They see Jesus as an important member of our family. Spending time in God's presence has brought on a sense of closeness for my family and I.

Time is the currency in any relationship; we can't invest in a relationship without giving our time.

1 Timothy 4:8

"Spiritual exercise is much more important and is a tonic for all you do. So exercise yourself spiritually, and practice being a better Christian because that will help you not only now in this life, but in the next life too."

Drawing into God's Love

"I have loved you with an everlasting love; I have drawn you with unfailing kindness" - Jeremiah 31:3

In the Message Bible version, Jeremiah's words are expressed as a promise to us, "I've never quit loving you and never will. Expect love, love, and more love". Experiencing God's love day after day is amazing; it restores our identity, makes us secure, is full of grace and is sustaining. There is nothing that can separate us from the love of God and that's a promise that can't be broken. God gives us great strength when required, wisdom and character to overcome our struggles as every day is an opportunity to meet with Jesus.

How to know more about God

As communication is essential for relationships to grow and good listening habits are key to finding out a lot about the other person, so is cultivating daily habits of reading the Bible help us to grow. It allows God to reveal what pleases Him through His living Word.

I can't imagine leaving my home in the morning without talking to my husband or children. Some mornings, I have a good catch up with my children on how we expect the day to be and at other times, I say a quick good morning and tell them I love them. It is very rare for me to leave my home without saying a word to anyone. Such it is that I have become more conscious of the intimacy that I have with God.

Love provides the absolute security that we need when we are in a fully trusting relationship. When we engage in regular active dialogue with God, we don't need to wait for the scary moments to press the panic button because we have established a routine of talking to God every day.

Philippians 4:6-7

6.   "Don't worry about anything; instead, pray about everything. Tell God what you need, and thank him for all he has done.

7.   Then you will experience God's peace, which exceeds anything we can understand. His peace will guard your hearts and minds as you live in Christ Jesus".

Prior to August 2015, I would have described my relationship with God as good. I was growing in my faith, experiencing miracles and had some stability in my life. I was also very busy looking after my home, raising my young children, juggling a career and keeping in touch with family and friends. But I didn't have the deep peace and joy that came with God's blessings.

I worried about everything; I worried about my children, my job, my home, my family, and friends. I read some passages in the Bible during my quiet time but couldn't relate to the message in a personal way. For instance, I felt I could no longer relate to Philippians 4:7. "Then you will experience God's peace, which exceeds anything we can understand. His peace will guard your hearts and minds as you live in Christ Jesus."

Worrying much implied that I didn't trust God's love to protect me. I concluded after a while, that it was not sustainable as a Christian to have a very long list of things to worry about, so I began to question my faith again. I knew God was real because I had called on him very many times and He answered me, but this time, I challenged myself whether I had gone cold, if there was intimacy in my relationship with God and if I really trusted Him.

In August 2015, I asked God to reveal more of Himself to me.

The Bible says in Jeremiah 29:13, "You will seek me and find me when you seek me with all your heart."

This wasn't the first time that I asked the Holy Spirit for help but it was the first time I was activating God's partnership to accomplish things I knew I couldn't do on my own, the things I worried about. I wanted the Word of God to soothe every anxiety I had and to really believe in the Bible verses I had read.

I decided to fast for 30 days to get myself in the right place so that I might have fewer distractions. I read my Bible, prayed, sat still and waited to hear from God. As each week went by, I heard nothing and so I would cut something else from my routine. I continued until I had one more week to go, then a few days left and I became desperate to hear from God.

In the last few days, I changed my routine completely and started asking questions again. What would God expect from me? I had been very focused on myself. At that precise moment, the Holy Spirit said, "Worship". That was something I hadn't incorporated into my routine.

I spent the next day in praise and worship. I began singing some of my favourite hymns and after a few hours, I felt my singing had changed a note. My singing had evolved to praising God and with each song I felt closer to God.

This happened for a few more hours and then I noticed again that my songs of praise had taken a different note and I was worshipping God. I can't really explain what happened next but I started to cry and the spirit of God came down. The room was very hot and bright and I fell to the floor as the Holy Spirit filled me with more and more of God's love.

Then I heard God speak to me. He slowly started to speak into the things I was most worried about. He told me that my children were going to be fine, my husband was going to be fine. God was reaffirming His love and speaking clearly to me about my family's safety. I was a bit confused because His words were reassuring me like I needed to hear it over and over again. I wondered what was going on. What about me? Was I going to be safe?

This happened over a three-day period and I became convinced that my assignment on earth was complete that finally, my soul had finally found Christ; I had finally seen God and it was finished.

But each day, The Holy Spirit poured out more of God's love into me and all I did was cry. I thought I was going to die. In a way, I wanted to be with the Father; the supernatural power of God's love was that strong. Heaven became real and very close. I told my husband something was happening (inside of me) that I couldn't explain.

I went to bed one evening after these encounters and I had a dream. I saw this picture which represented my life, it was a canvas painting with loads of colours which was being wiped clean, the hand movement continued until all the colours disappeared till it turned to a plain white canvas. Suddenly all the plans I had seemed to disappear.

Each time, I thought that was it; that my life was over and I was leaving this world. I cried on the side; tears flowing down my cheeks but I couldn't explain why I was crying that much.

Then the Lord spoke to me:
My dear daughter,
Fear not, you will not die.
It is the Spirit that gives life.
The flesh is of no help.

The words I speak to you are spirit and life

You have an assignment to do for me so I have wiped all your plans

I have a better plan for you and I will prepare you for it.

I love you my dearest daughter

Papa

I instantly said "yes" to God, yes to His plans as I chose to put my trust in Him. Submitting to God's agenda is so liberating and experiencing his supernatural love caused me to stop worrying. I know that whatever plans the Lord has laid out for me to do, He will accomplish. I could now rest, not worrying about my future because I was drawn into God's love.

Points for Reflection

We need to rest in the presence of God with the full assurance that our heavenly father loves us dearly. We should allow our time of rest to be a place of trust that enables us to let go of our fears and replace it with a time of worship. In this special place, we cease from our own works of self-dependency, to go into His rest of God-dependency, trusting Him to take care of our every need.

INTIMACY WITH GOD

Prayer

Abba Father,

Thank You for Your everlasting love and the security I have in You that brings me eternal peace.

Your comforting words - "Be still and know I am Lord", is my song of worship as I totally surrender my all to You.

I cast my burdens and lay them at Your feet and in exchange, You've given me the freedom to dream as a child and to sleep at night with a smile on my face.

Your love overwhelms me as Your mighty hand protects me, You neither slumber nor sleep; day and night, You watch and preserve me.

You took me to a spacious place and there I rest without a care, so I boldly sing it is well and all my days will I worship you forever.

Amen

Chapter 3

Sufficiency in Christ

A Safe Tower

"The name of the Lord is a fortified tower; the righteous run to it and are safe"

- Proverbs 18:10

The key to the great promises of God is anchored in Jesus. Accepting God's love into our hearts creates a strong awareness of His presence. It becomes a tower of refuge where the saints run to and are safe.

When we become born again, we are sealed with the love of Christ. For some of us, it may take a while for that identity to take root in our minds and to stop doubting. This is because we find ourselves stumbling occasionally and our identity comes under attack by the accuser Satan. However, there is a defining moment when we become fully conscious of our identity and know that we are deeply rooted in God's love.

In God's presence, there is fullness of Joy and light radiates through. Satan is an outsider that is not invited to be in the presence of God. He is challenged as the door is shut in his face. He is very much aware of this transition phase and he knows that he has lost his grip on us. Therefore, the only tool available to him will be to distract us, disarm us and tempt us to come out of our safe tower.

Our intimacy with God during this period, becomes our shield because the Holy Spirit guides and equips us to spot the disguises of Satan. The Bible warns us that Satan comes like a thief in the night, he masks his face so no one will know him.

Job 24:14

"They are murderers who rise in the early dawn to kill the poor and needy; at night they are thieves and adulterers, waiting for the twilight 'when no one will see me,' they say. They mask their faces so no one will know them."

But those who know Jesus do not need to see, our spirit recognises His Voice.

John 10:27

"My sheep recognize my voice, and I know them, and they follow me..."

Following Christ protects us from the dangerous slopes and life's worries because Satan accuses us of every sin that there is at every opportunity and tells us that we can't live in the 'Garden of Eden'. Jesus says it is true that we can't enter God's presence in our old self but the price has been paid and we are free to enter the presence of God when we are born-again. As our devotion to God deepens, the temptation from Satan intensifies.

I looked at the dialogue between Jesus and Peter. Jesus told Peter that he will be the rock to build his church; Jesus affirmed Peter's identity.

Matthew 16:18

"And now I'm going to tell you who you are, really are. You are Peter, a rock. This is the rock on which I will put together my church..."

At the height of Peter's devotion to Christ, he said he was ready to go with him to prison and die. This is a profound place to be when our relationship is steadfast because we know Jesus intimately. We can make these bold statements, knowing He has the full authority to set us free.

Sadly, Peter fell at his first attempt, but Jesus' redeeming love for Peter saved him. Let's explore the model Jesus set for Peter to show us how we can re-affirm our identity in Christ when we find ourselves stepping outside the safe tower.

Luke 22: 31-33

31   "Simon, Simon, Satan has asked to have you, to sift you like wheat,

32   but I have pleaded in prayer for you that your faith

should not completely fail. So when you have repented and turned to me again, strengthen and build up the faith of your brothers."

33 Simon said, "Lord, I am ready to go to jail with you, and even to die with you."

Jesus was moved and at the same time, He had deep compassion for Peter. He was familiar with this situation. Jesus said, "Satan has asked to sift all of you as wheat". This is similar to what Job experienced, as Satan accuses all of us that our love for Christ is conditional, meaning, we love God because of the security that we have in the safe tower. This doesn't matter; God said that we love because He first loved us.

Jesus reaffirmed His love to Peter and His response was full of grace. "I have prayed for you that your faith may not fail. And when you have turned back, strengthen your brothers." We read later that Peter denied Jesus three times shortly after his moment of affirmation and wept bitterly when it happened. However, Peter recovered from this incident and fulfilled the destiny that Christ had for him.

Our identity and relationship is secure in Christ. Like Peter, we may fail, we may fall but Jesus tells us to repent quickly and run back to the safe place, His dwelling where Satan can't come in. Over time, as we draw close to God, we will get better at spotting the fake and disarming our distractions.

People may come to us in the name of God, but we should be bold to ask,"which god?" because there are very many gods today but it is only one God that offers us an everlasting love. We should check that it is God Almighty, His son Jesus Christ and the Holy Spirit. God's love satisfies and is indestructible.

Therefore, reviewing the model from Peter's example, there are three main lessons we can learn from:

Lesson 1: When we move away from His Presence, we should find a way to pray...

Luke 22: 32 says, "... but I have pleaded in prayer for you that your faith should not completely fail..."

When trials and temptations occur or events that are out of our control happen, our hope in Christ becomes our shield. David who was one of the greatest kings of Israel and who God described as a man after His heart, cried out to God, amid his trials. Psalm 119:114 - "You are my refuge and my shield; I have put my hope in your word". We can be deep in God's love, and still face some of our greatest challenges.

Here is another story of momentarily stepping out of God's tower.

After a refilling of the Holy Spirit, my heart was full of joy; I was like a new bride again and enjoyed great intimacy talking to God. Several miracles happened in a short period of time, fuelled by my faith because I simply believed. I had occasional challenges but they weren't strong enough to uproot my deep roots. It is a lovely place to be; I had deep peace in my heart and no longer became worried.

But things changed abruptly, without any warning. In a short period of time, three weeks to be precise, I lost two loved ones that were precious to me. One was unexpected because I had seen my friend the day before. We met up and had an amazing time together, laughing and making plans for the coming months. She was involved in an accident the next day and was gone so soon. I was unprepared for the news. This was the first time I faced the call of death in a way that pierced my heart; my pain changed to disbelief and I became quite upset.

I couldn't understand why God hadn't hinted that this was going to happen, I prayed every day and spoke to Him, why was this kept from me? The loss was unbearable but I knew I couldn't abandon my faith. Jesus was real, He had done many things in my life so it wasn't an option nor did I consider leaving my faith.

Whilst contemplating my loss, shortly after, I lost my grandmother who I was very close to, coupled with a series of other unexpected events occurring at the same time and the combination of these trials threw me off guard. My faith was vigorously being shaken like a hurricane wind and I fell sick after being run down.

The right response would have been to run to God. However, facing God in this circumstance was difficult and challenging.

There was a war going on in my head. I finally summoned the courage to go to church even though my mind was disconnected. At the time, my pain was still so raw, I couldn't sing the hymns, some of the songs were too painful, and the lyrics threw me off. It reminded me of the Bible verses I read with my head but found difficult to connect with in my heart.

Then the talk started and the preacher gave a sermon on the parable of the lost sheep found in Luke 15 verses 1-7. As the talk progressed, I got more upset and started asking questions again. Why was God running after the lost sheep, why was that more important than the ninety-nine sheep left to fend on their own.

As the war of words continued in my head, I switched off from the sermon and sat still. Then the gentlest whisper came into my heart and I heard the Holy Spirit say the words I had been aching to hear, "Sorry".

As soon as I heard the words, at that precise moment, the Holy Spirit cancelled every voice in my head and reconciled my peace with God. I broke down in tears. It was so important to know that God knew of my pain, I couldn't express in words how I felt. Accepting God's love at a critical moment was important.

When my heart began to respond again to God, the Holy Spirit asked me to pick up my Bible to address the question I had, which was, "What happens to the ninety-nine other sheep?" I read Luke 15 again, but to the end. This time, it was the story of the prodigal son, but the focus was on the older son, the good son.

Luke 15: 28-32

28   "The older brother became angry and refused to go in. So his father went out and pleaded with him.

29.   But he answered his father, 'Look! All these years I've been slaving for you and never disobeyed your orders. Yet you never gave me even a young goat so I could celebrate with my friends

30.   But when this son of yours who has squandered your property with prostitutes comes home, you kill the fattened calf for him!'

31.   "'My son,' the father said, 'you are always with me, and everything I have is yours.

32.   But we had to celebrate and be glad, because this brother of yours was dead and is alive again; he was lost and is found."

The story of the prodigal son illustrates how with the two brothers, we can move away from God's presence sometimes only momentarily and other times, it may seem like a decade.

God loves us very much and would never want us to step out of His presence even for a second. However, when we step out, His loving grace will do what it takes to bring us in if we soften our hearts to God. Intimacy with Christ, to hear Him clearly, is vital to weather the storms when they appear. It establishes our identity in Christ and allows our roots to grow even deeper.

Lesson 2: Mend your heart and return to God

Luke 22: 32 says, "So when you have repented and turned to me again…"

Just like the father in the Prodigal Son story in Luke 15, God is yearning for us to turn to Him in order that He might take us up in His arms and embrace us for the rest of our lives. He is not expecting us to do everything possible to get to Him or bend over backwards, He just wants us to turn our hearts towards Him today.

God's amazing grace is freely available to everyone, especially to those who are lost, withdrawn or appear stagnant in their relationship with God.

Luke 19:10

"For the Son of Man came to seek and to save the lost."

Jesus knows of all our struggles and taught us a simple prayer to connect with God daily, which helps us to be right in our hearts so that we may experience God's good love.

The Lord's Prayer

Matthew 6: 9-13 NKJV

Our Father in heaven,

Hallowed be Your name.

Your kingdom come.

Your will be done
On earth as it is in heaven.
Give us this day our daily bread.
And forgive us our debts,
As we forgive our debtors.
And do not lead us into temptation,
But deliver us from the evil one.
For Yours is the kingdom and the power and the glory forever.
Amen.

Honouring God daily and asking for His daily bread, the bread of life purifies our heart. Turning over our lives to Christ should become a daily habit that we choose to do consciously; it's a way to guard ourselves against the schemes of Satan.

We need to remain watchful because Satan will always attempt to steal the word and disguise what our Father meant for good and turn it into despair. He does this by sending agents with lying spirits and accuses us of our sins to stop us from mending our hearts. Therefore, the Word of God becomes our shield in these times, as Jesus constantly assures us of who we are and rebukes Satan for us.

John 8:44

"He has always hated the truth, because there is no truth in him. When he lies, it is consistent with his character; for he is a liar and the father of lies."

Turning back to God isn't complicated because Jesus has already paid the high price of our sin. His death on the cross enables all of us to have this open grace to repent in our heart.

Here is a story I like which reflects keeping it simple:

2 Kings 5: 9-15

9.   "So Naaman went with his horses and chariots and waited at the door of Elisha's house.

10.   But Elisha sent a messenger out to him with this message: "Go and wash yourself seven times in the Jordan River. Then your skin will be restored, and you will be healed of your leprosy."

11.   But Naaman became angry and stalked away. "I thought he would certainly come out to meet me!" he said. "I expected him to wave his hand over the leprosy and call on the name of the Lord his God and heal me!

12.   Aren't the rivers of Damascus, the Abana and the Pharpar, better than any of the rivers of Israel? Why shouldn't I wash in them and be healed?" So Naaman turned and went away in a rage.

13.   But his officers tried to reason with him and said, "Sir, if the prophet had told you to do something very difficult, wouldn't you have done it? So you should certainly obey him when he says simply, 'Go and wash and be cured!'"

14.   So Naaman went down to the Jordan River and dipped himself seven times, as the man of God had instructed him. And his skin became as healthy as the skin of a young child, and he was healed!"

Whenever I find myself stepping away from God's presence and relying on my own strength to achieve something, I revaluate, STOP and reset my agenda. I heard a wonderful sermon by Ken Costa about leaning on the promises of the Word rather than the premises of the world. He explained that stepping away and doing it our way leads to disaster but God's way always leads to victory.

When we place our plans in God's hands, our potter, we begin to rest in His presence. God's grace and mercy overrides everything. Even when we are stubborn and momentarily move away from God's presence, He catches us when we fall.

Jeremiah uses the story of the potter's house to explain how important our life is to God. I watched a YouTube video on pottering to help me visualise this art. Each time the clay fell or shaped itself in a slightly unusual way, the potter, already knowing the end state would keep moulding the clay until it was made perfect.

The potter transformed an ugly lump of clay into beautiful pottery. Each touch made it more complete and it is comforting to see that the clay is always in the potter's hand, just like God shapes us; never leaving or forsaking us.

At the Potter's House

Jeremiah 18:1-10

1.   "This is the word that came to Jeremiah from the Lord:

2.   Go down to the potter's house, and there I will give you

my message.'

3. So I went down to the potter's house, and I saw him working at the wheel.

4. But the pot he was shaping from the clay was marred in his hands; so the potter formed it into another pot, shaping it as seemed best to him.

5. Then the word of the Lord came to me.

6. He said, 'Can I not do with you, Israel, as this potter does?' declares the Lord. 'Like clay in the hand of the potter, so are you in my hand, Israel.

7. If at any time I announce that a nation or kingdom is to be uprooted, torn down and destroyed,

8. And if that nation I warned repents of its evil, then I will relent and not inflict on it the disaster I had planned.

9. And if at another time I announce that a nation or kingdom is to be built up and planted.

10. And if it does evil in my sight and does not obey me, then I will reconsider the good I had intended to do for it.

Lesson 3: Strengthen yourself in the faith

Luke 22:32 says, "...strengthen and build up the faith of your brothers."

Isaiah 41:10

"Do not fear, for I am with you.

Do not be afraid, for I am your God.

I will give you strength, and for sure I will help you.

Yes, I will hold you up with My right hand that is right and good."

Our relationship with God is very personal and God's love is unique to each person. God says He loves us so much that He sent Jesus, His only son, to die for us. My vicar, Nicky Gumbel, at Holy Trinity Brompton, often says during the Alpha course, "If I were the only person on this earth, Jesus would still have come to die for me."

Death is one of the fiercest hurricanes that we will ever face and this can come to reality when confronted with the loss of a loved one. It is one life event that we can't prepare for but our relationship with Christ allows us to cope with it because Christ Himself demonstrated His love by dying for us.

Romans 5:8

"But God demonstrates his own love for us in this: While we were still sinners, Christ died for us."

I have read the above verse in the past without making a full connection with it in my heart because I hadn't until recently experienced death in a personal way. So, when I found myself in this difficult period, I needed to shut the door and keep my eyes on God. I looked to Jesus to deal with this.

I reflected on the Bible passage in Mark 5, below, to help guide me on how to depend on His grace at a tough period.

SUFFICIENCY IN CHRIST

Mark 5: 35- 43

35.   "While he was still speaking to her, messengers arrived from the home of Jairus, the leader of the synagogue. They told him, "Your daughter is dead. There's no use troubling the Teacher now.

36.   But Jesus overheard them and said to Jairus, "Don't be afraid. Just have faith."

37.   Then Jesus stopped the crowd and wouldn't let anyone go with him except Peter, James, and John (the brother of James).

38.   When they came to the home of the synagogue leader, Jesus saw much commotion and weeping and wailing.

39.   He went inside and asked, "Why all this commotion and weeping? The child isn't dead; she's only asleep."

40.   The crowd laughed at him. But he made them all leave, and he took the girl's father and mother and his three disciples into the room where the girl was lying.

41.   Holding her hand, he said to her, "Talitha koum," which means "Little girl, get up!"

42.   And the girl, who was twelve years old, immediately stood up and walked around! They were overwhelmed and totally amazed.

43.   Jesus gave them strict orders not to tell anyone what had happened, and then he told them to give her something to eat."

From the story, I saw a pattern to follow:

-     Jesus told Jairus to have faith – don't listen to the crowd.

- Jesus stopped the crowd from coming further - your cry for help is an individual cry.

- Jesus shut the door – sometimes you have to stand alone with God when those around do not understand.

Spending more time reading the Bible helped me to cope during my strengthening period. When the storm came, I turned off the books, the daily devotionals and ran with both hands to equip myself with the living word of God.

Hebrews 6:19

"We who have run for our very lives to God have every reason to grab the promised hope with both hands and never let go. It's an unbreakable spiritual lifeline, reaching past all appearances right to the very presence of God where Jesus, running on ahead of us, has taken up his permanent post as high priest for us."

We must open our hearts to God because any words of wisdom that we receive from friends during our trial periods would seem like parables until God opens our eyes. Our family and friends' words of wisdom may console us but it is God's word that penetrates our soul.

God speaks to us directly, in a way that our spirit understands. The peace of God floods our lives and we are comforted in an unexplainable way that our natural minds can't fathom. In my case, I had to shut the door to hear Him clearly.

Here is another story, this time from Elisha:

2 Kings 4: 2-6

2. "What can I do to help you?" Elisha asked. "Tell me, what do you have in the house?" "Nothing at all, except a flask of olive oil," she replied.

3. And Elisha said, "Borrow as many empty jars as you can from your friends and neighbours.

4. Then go into your house with your sons and shut the door behind you. Pour olive oil from your flask into the jars, setting each one aside when it is filled.

5. So she did as she was told. Her sons kept bringing jars to her, and she filled one after another

6. Soon every container was full to the brim! "Bring me another jar," she said to one of her sons. "There aren't any more!" he told her. And then the olive oil stopped flowing."

When God instructs us to stretch our faith in an unthinkable manner, we need to shut the door so that our faith won't waiver when the world laughs and mocks us. Some people may have good intentions but their words may not align with what God wants to do for us. We must remember that they can't see the soul and therefore are unable to help in desperate situations that require great faith.

At other times, people unknowingly do the opposite of lifting us up. They fuel the noise levels in our situation as they tell us, statistically, what's never been done or provide answers based on what they see. Our God defies statistics and human wisdom; He can work with nothing, for with God all things are possible.

We need to have our personal stories, our 'Red Sea' miracles, so that our faith can be strengthened and anchored in Christ. These miracles are intended to strengthen us but never for self-gratification.

My God is the same yesterday, today and forever. The true source of our strength comes from God and hearing the word of God. The Bible is the living word of God. This book and every book we read should never substitute the word of God. They are our stories testifying on God's goodness to strengthen us in our faith, not to replace the Bible.

Christ Alone is Sufficient

"Do not harden your hearts, "Today, if you hear his voice, do not harden your hearts as you did in the rebellion."
- Hebrew 3:15

Jesus Christ is all we need when things appear a bit shaky and so I opened my heart to God during my strengthening period. I benefited immensely from my quiet times, my resting times - praying, listening and singing hymns. I was plugged in to Heaven and the peace of God sustained me.

My primary need was God's comfort and the physical manifestation of answers to prayers was secondary. It allowed me to depend more on God for His outcome and not what I wanted, as His outcome will be better than what I had imagined. I was content being in the safe tower and taking it back to basics, enjoying the things God had provided to me.

I learnt over time, to avoid the mistake of asking to see miracles happen before reconnecting to God, instead, I now repent and go to God. I had heard some people say that they don't see biblical miracles in our present day and as a result they stay lukewarm. When they say these things, they limit the power of God in their personal lives.

The questions we ought to ask are: Do we know God personally? Do we love God with all our heart and do we obey His commands? If we make way for God in our personal lives, we won't need to compare the miracles of yesterday to today. Instead, we would look inward and know that God has indeed satisfied our innermost longing to be one with Him.

For those who ask these questions, Jesus' response is in Matthew 16: 1- 19. Read this story in your Bible or go online to search for it. It is important that you read the Holy Bible's reference to this to independently receive Truth.

The passage focuses on the religious leaders (not the common man) asking Jesus for more miracles. They asked Him to show great demonstrations from heaven to prove His authority. Jesus retorted that the sinful people of those days go after something special to see. "There will be nothing special for them to see except the miracle that happened to Jonah." He said and He went away from them.

We are blessed today to know that Christ rose from the dead after three days so that the similarities in the prophecy relating to Jonah being in the whale's tummy for three days came to pass; although the people in Matthew 16 didn't see it come to pass. They were not looking or seeking for Christ. If we find ourselves asking God for great demonstrations during our strengthening period, we should reflect on this passage.

There were times in the Bible when God performed miracles to equip and strengthen individuals for a task. These miracles were intended to equip the individual to put their trust in God. Ultimately, it is Jesus who answers the questions during the strengthening period and gives us His peace.

Jesus told his disciples to be careful of the wrong teachings of the Pharisees because great miracles do not answer the important questions in life, instead Jesus turned to His disciples and asked, "Who do you think I am?"

Matthew 16: 16-17

16.   "Simon Peter answered, "You are the Messiah, the Son of the living God."

17.   Jesus replied, "You are blessed, Simon son of John, because my Father in heaven has revealed this to you. You did not learn this from any human being."

During the strengthening period, the Lord may ask us to shut the door so that God can reveal who He is in us. I often say to myself, "I am who I am because of who He is." Our salvation, faith and hope, should be anchored on our personal relationship with Christ. He alone is sufficient. If we ever find ourselves shaken or doing the unthinkable or unimaginable; may I suggest closing the door quietly behind you and talk to God.

Matthew 6:6

"Jesus said, "But when you pray, go away by yourself, shut the door behind you, and pray to your Father in private. Then your Father, who sees everything, will reward you".

Let's avoid the temptation of seeking the promises of God before a relationship. Otherwise, we would become like those who rejected Christ, yet were waiting for a king to free them from oppression; unless this freedom came, He wasn't their Messiah.

Matthew 27:40

"Look at you now!" they yelled at him. "You said you were going to destroy the Temple and rebuild it in three days. Well then, if you are the Son of God, save yourself and come down from the cross!"

We shouldn't associate who the Messiah is by the things we see or let our expectations, thoughts or feelings consume our thinking, as they draw our attention away from our relationship with God. We need to worship God in spirit and truth before the blessings come.

2 Corinthians 13:5

"Paul said examine yourselves to see if your faith is genuine. Test yourselves. Surely you know that Jesus Christ is among you; if not, you have failed the test of genuine faith."

The Lord says rejoice always as if we have those things now – our faith is evidence of things not seen; yet we rejoice in the Lord. Our true promise is our heavenly reward. Christ is all we need.

2 Peter 1:3

"For as you know him better, he will give you, through his great power, everything you need for living a truly good life..."

Points for Reflection

We should accept the gift of our salvation and be fully confident that Jesus has paid a very high price for our sins. He is the perfect sacrifice removing all our guilt and shame, by replacing it with robes of righteousness. Therefore, whenever we find ourselves going through our trials, we should remember that Jesus has defeated Satan and He is our Shepherd watching over us.

SUFFICIENCY IN CHRIST

Prayer

Dear Jesus,
I look back at what You have done for me and I say thank You.
Thank You, everlasting Father, the One who sees and hears my cries.

Thank You for Your grace, Your protection and love.

Thank You for providing a shelter for me; a strong tower away from my enemies.

Thank You for lifting me up at the right time for You said there is a season for everything.

You are my potter; You moulded me all through the years and each time I strayed, You embraced me like a prodigal child and told me You love me.

You reset my plans and shaped me to fulfil Your perfect plans for me.

I don't know tomorrow but I know You Lord and because You live, I can face tomorrow.

I look forward to my glorious future where one day, I shall be with You.

Keep me till then and may You never leave nor forsake me.
Amen.

Part II

Part II

Chapter 4

My Story

She said "Yes!"

"Jesus replied, "With all the earnestness I possess I tell you this: Unless you are born again, you can never get into the Kingdom of God."

- John 3:5

I became a born-again Christian in April 2000 and I still find it quite fascinating that I can remember the precise day, hour and time. It's still quite vivid in my memory and I am thankful for this.

Isn't it strange that we don't know what it must have felt like to be born other than the fact that we must have cried a lot on the day. Maybe the clue is in the crying; there is something to be said for feeling detached from God and having to come to earth.

Neither will we know personally what it will feel like when we pass on but I can imagine that most of us will have loved ones crying because they'll miss us yet at the same time, they'll also be rejoicing that we are back in Heaven.

However, for one moment, I am thankful to have experienced and remembered the day I became born-again, spiritually born of Christ. And yes, I did cry when it happened. So how did it happen? This is a good time to tell why and how I made the decision to commit my life spiritually to Jesus.

I have always considered myself a Christian; however, I was not born again. Whenever I met born again Christians, they appeared to be fanatics, extreme in their thinking and unrelatable so I shied away from anything extreme. I wasn't excessive in anyway, I went to school, had friends and was happy. I went to church occasionally, usually at special events; however, we often had a lie in on Sundays to rest.

There were times in church, where the sermon was uplifting and sometimes provoking and whenever there was an altar call, I responded by giving my life to Christ and repenting (obviously with no real understanding). I must have gone forward at least ten times but got closer at each stage with the understanding of what grace meant. I understood that Christ died once and for all but just to be sure I still went forward. I had rationalised this by thinking that I was often good and sometimes bad.

I made sure my (good) credits outweighed my bad deeds and if I was in the positive, I was ok. With this mindset, I found it difficult to be a Christian. At the time, I felt it was all about obeying rules and I found religion a bit restrictive; however, given that I had the fear of God, I would never deny that there wasn't a God.

Consequently, I however had several questions playing in my head, perhaps I didn't believe God was a good God and thought that He ultimately makes us pay for our sins. I also thought, "Why is there evil in world? Why do innocent children die? Why do parents of young children die?" These questions piled up in my heart and created a barrier and over the years, this barrier grew into a very tall wall.

My sister and I moved to Leeds and I noticed that she had started going more regularly to church and something was a bit different this time. She appeared much calmer and more at peace with herself.

I can't remember if she ever spoke to me directly about God or just that she had found this fantastic church, Bridge Street and had asked me to come with her. I found myself going to church this Sunday in April 2000. I can still remember the message even after many years have gone by. It was Nehemiah 4 verses 1-7.

Nehemiah 4: 1-7

1.   "Sanballat was very angry when he learned that we were rebuilding the wall. He flew into a rage and mocked the Jews,

2.   Saying in front of his friends and the Samarian army officers, "What does this bunch of poor, feeble Jews think they're doing? Do they think they can build the

wall in a single day by just offering a few sacrifices? Do they actually think they can make something of stones from a rubbish heap—and charred ones at that?"

3.   Tobiah the Ammonite, who was standing beside him, remarked, "That stone wall would collapse if even a fox walked along the top of it!"

4.   Then I prayed, "Hear us, our God, for we are being mocked. May their scoffing fall back on their own heads, and may they themselves become captives in a foreign land!

5.   Do not ignore their guilt. Do not blot out their sins, for they have provoked you to anger here in front of the builders."

6.   At last the wall was completed to half its height around the entire city, for the people had worked with enthusiasm."

This Word pierced my heart and sliced it right through. Was I a Christian or not? I was an occasional churchgoer but could I answer the question with such certainty. It was addressing the fact that I was work in progress; perhaps a feeble Christian made from a pile of rubbish and if people threw stones at it, perhaps my foundations would crumble.

The Scripture went further in verse 6 that the wall was completed to half its height and God still loves me. For the first time, I heard that God takes us from where we are and completes us if we let Him. Sin was common to man and it was God who restores. It was a powerful sermon, which concluded that the wall was completed.

MY STORY

Nehemiah 6:15-16

15.   "So on October 2, the wall was finished—just fifty-two days after we had begun.

16.   When our enemies and the surrounding nations heard about it, they were frightened and humiliated. They realized this work had been done with the help of our God.

I never went forward after that day for altar calls because the Holy Spirit had sealed it in my heart once and for all, that I was a child of God. I took the extra step and went on the Alpha course. The course is designed for anyone who has questions about the Christian faith. I enrolled on this course to explore the questions I had and to discover the meaning of life. This course helped to restore my spiritual walls.

Since then, my walk with God has gone from half built to what it is now and each day I have added extra bricks and continue to do so. Stones have been thrown, some bricks have fallen and been put back again but now the temple is firmly secured.

This is my story and I'm sure everyone has their story. Our response to God's love affects how we relate to others. He transforms us so that by our actions, we too can radiate light as He gives us the boldness to tell others.

Thank God that some people took the time to write to us about God's love, as the Bible; A story about God's rescue mission and grace, a story of great faith, all of which have encouraged me in my walk with God. I thank God for sending Jesus, our role model and for using ordinary lives like Nehemiah, David, Joseph, Moses, Abraham, Paul, Matthew, Mark, Luke, John, Esther and Ruth to show His great power to turn things around.

It is for this reason that I've written my story; I'm just an ordinary person experiencing God's great love.

My Special Song:

You are great
You are faithful
You restore hope
You are light
You are my Living Water
You are joy
You are wonderful
You are God
You are Jehovah
You are Saviour
You are Redeemer
You are great in battle
You are Mighty Warrior
You are gentle
You are wise
You are the Lamb of God
You are the Lion of Judah
You are awesome
I call you Abba Father

Chapter 5

Purpose

Proverbs 1: 1-7

The Purpose of Proverbs

1. "These are the proverbs of Solomon, David's son, king of Israel.

2. Their purpose is to teach people wisdom and discipline, to help them understand the insights of the wise.

3. Their purpose is to teach people to live disciplined and successful lives, to help them do what is right, just, and fair.

4. These proverbs will give insight to the simple, knowledge and discernment to the young.

5. Let the wise listen to these proverbs and become even wiser. Let those with understanding receive guidance

6. By exploring the meaning in these proverbs and parables, the words of the wise and their riddles.

7. Fear of the Lord is the foundation of true knowledge, but fools despise wisdom and discipline."

Defining our purpose can be one of the most abstract questions we can ask. We can fake it and give an answer that may seem right just to show others that we have it all figured out. I was once asked at a graduate fair years ago what my ambition and purpose was. I answered, "to help solve world peace and work for the United Nations". I gave a sincerely genuine response because at that time I thought I could do my part to help solve a tiny piece of the world's issues. Needless to say, this was not quite how it turned out years later.

I ended up working in Financial Services, perhaps the opposite end of what society would consider a noble profession. According to a survey in 2008, bankers are the third least trusted profession in the UK, beaten only by journalists and politicians. I must put a caveat here that there are a quite a few noble people who work in what may seem like less noble professions. But, I won't digress on the topic, as I gave this example to show that understanding what purpose is as a student, is almost as vague as asking what is the meaning of life?

So, when I started writing on this topic, I researched what experts had to say with having a sense of purpose. One such article was published in Psychology today (https://www.psychologytoday.com/blog/out-the darkness/201307/the-power-purpose). It said that the need for purpose is one of the defining characteristics of human beings. Human beings crave purpose, and suffer serious psychological difficulties when they don't have it. Purpose is a fundamental component of a fulfilling life.

PURPOSE

If understanding our purpose is so fundamental to our outlook in life, then it certainly is worth exploring what it is and how it affects us. As this book centres on God, I've cut right through this subject, not to discuss the divergent opinions on what purpose is but to focus solely on a God-centred purpose. I therefore think that it makes sense to find out what God says.

Ecclesiastes 12: 13

"Let us hear the conclusion of the whole matter: Fear God, and keep his commandments: for this is the whole duty of man."

Jeremiah 32: 39- 41

39. "And I will give them one heart and one purpose: to worship me forever, for their own good and for the good of all their descendants.

40. And I will make an everlasting covenant with them: I will never stop doing good for them. I will put a desire in their hearts to worship me, and they will never leave me.

41. I will find joy doing good for them and will faithfully and wholeheartedly replant them in this land.

Ephesians 1:11

"It's in Christ that we find out who we are and what we are living for. Long before we first heard of Christ and got our hopes up, he had his eye on us, had designs on us for glorious living, part of the overall purpose he is working out in everything and everyone."

Rick Warren did a fantastic job in his book, The Purpose Driven Life, to explain what a godly purpose is. He says that the starting place to answer this question must be with God. He states that if we believe that God created us, then it would be quite challenging as created beings to know our purpose without asking the inventor.

Likewise, I am convinced that we can't fully understand the depth of our purpose or why we are here until we are connected with God in a fully trusting and loving relationship. I believe our eternal purpose of why we exist is to enjoy God's love.

A quote from Michael Houdmann's book, Got Questions, summarises this nicely. It says that our purpose in life, as it was when God originally created man in the book of Genesis was to:

· Glorify God and enjoy fellowship with Him
· Have good relationships with others
· Work
· Have dominion over the earth

But with man's fall into sin, fellowship with God is broken, relationships with others are strained, work seems to always be frustrating, and man struggles to maintain any semblance of dominion over nature. Only by restoring fellowship with God, through faith in Jesus Christ, can purpose in life be rediscovered.

PURPOSE

Our purpose is to glorify God and enjoy Him forever; this we ought to do by building our core spiritual muscle to worship Him daily. Our journey is an eternal one as we fix our eyes on our future home in Heaven and know Him intimately.

Purpose transcends everything; it strikes at the core of who we are, why we were created and leads the way for us to be transformed to be more like Christ.

Multi-Faceted Purpose

We enjoy God by following His purpose for our lives, which enables us to experience true and lasting joy, the abundant life that He desires for us. As I developed my relationship with God and my intimacy with Him grew, suddenly, I discovered that I was created with far greater abilities than I had imagined because God's grace has no limit.

Psalm 119:96

"Your commands are boundless."

My purpose wasn't to be defined in a tangible way but rather in an infinite boundless way that allowed me to evolve as God intended.

My purpose was centred on God.
- I was created to worship God
- I was created to love and fear God
- I was created to enjoy all His creations
- I was created to live for God
- I was created to excel

I had defined my purpose by what I enjoyed doing and relied on indicators of what I had achieved so far to validate it. However, achieving good merits like a rewarding career or a good education, without a foundation in Jesus Christ, left me with a void yet to be filled.

I am thankful that my feelings of emptiness disappeared after discovering Christ. I often read in newspapers, stories of successful people who take their lives after years of misery. These stories often have a shock factor as these individuals appeared to have had it all, success, fame and money. Jesus does not promise us a life of misery but rather He promises us a very rewarding life, He is the true source of joy.

John 10:10
"The thief comes only in order to steal and kill and destroy. I came that they may have and enjoy life, and have it in abundance [to the full, till it overflows]."

The void we sometimes feel can only be filled by connecting with Jesus and others. It is love centred. Love activates our purpose beyond our personal accomplishments. It activates our desire to be in constant fellowship with God and takes responsibilities for the people He has placed in our care. This results in us living diligently and seeing situations as Jesus would – having compassion and bringing joy to those around us.

Therefore, I retuned my mind to accept my purpose in living for Christ in all that I did. In whatever role I played - wife, mother, daughter, sister, friend, student, colleague, employer, church volunteer, mentor; knowing that I can do all things and be filled with joy. My joy is more amplified when these activities allow me to connect with Christ.

When I realised that my purpose can be multi-faceted, it took out a lot of barriers than I had envisioned. For instance, when I gave my first public talk in a church, I was nervous. I thought to myself, "I'm not a preacher and worse still, I'm not in the right frame of mind." Think of the story of Jonah when God asked him to go to Nineveh and you'll get a clear picture of where I was.

It was at my lowest point that God had called me to give my first public talk. It was mind boggling, but I was filled with God's love that telling others about Him was more important than my state of mind and I jumped at the opportunity.

Even in unfamiliar territory, our trust in God enables us to go beyond what we think our abilities are because we know that He is a good God. Therefore, it was very important for me to retune my faith and believe in all things that God is a good God. Without this fundamental belief, my purpose in accomplishing greater things was restricted by fear.

When the fear of failure disappears, we are free to live. Just like an innocent child playing in the park, catches a glimpse of her father watching over her, is free to run in the open field with that assurance.

I had limited my purpose to my capabilities but now I am more convinced that our purpose extends beyond where we are right now. If individuals can have multiple interests that can be so diverse, how much more we that have the added advantage of being in Christ. We can achieve our assignments with a godly purpose and are more than able to evolve and develop wherever God plants us.

Jeremiah 32:41

"I will find joy doing good for them and will faithfully and wholeheartedly replant them in this land."

My prayer is that we release our faith to reach the full potential of what He has in store for us. The Holy Spirit will reveal to us our assignments and we should depend on God to equip us with special gifts and abilities to complete each one. With the power of the Holy Spirit, we can do all things through Christ. God has given us special and distinct abilities to fulfil His plans.

I came to rest in my understanding that my purpose is embedded in God's love and in any assignment that I do, which impacts others in a positive way, I am rest assured that my Father in heaven will be cheering for me to succeed.

So, I settled with the decision in my heart that my purpose here on earth is to worship God for it was intended for man to be in constant fellowship with God and look after all His creations.

PURPOSE

We are Salt and Light

Matthew 5: 13-16

13   "Let me tell you why you are here. You're here to be salt-seasoning that brings out the God-flavours of this earth. If you lose your saltiness, how will people taste godliness? You've lost your usefulness and will end up in the garbage.

14-16   "Here's another way to put it: You're here to be light, bringing out the God-colours in the world. God is not a secret to be kept. We're going public with this, as public as a city on a hill. If I make you light-bearers, you don't think I'm going to hide you under a bucket, do you? I'm putting you on a light stand. Now that I've put you there on a hilltop, on a light stand—shine! Keep open house; be generous with your lives. By opening up to others, you'll prompt people to open up with God, this generous Father in heaven.

In Christ, we have a godly purpose that drives our actions. Jesus says that we are the salt of the earth, the world's light for all to see. Having been born again, the Holy Spirit gives us a new identity and a new purpose. Suddenly, we are pushed out so that the world may see Christ in us.

We are transformed into the image of Christ and we now radiate light to the chaotic world that is around us. In fact, we are here to save the world, by leading people to Christ. Through their salvation, they will have an everlasting life beyond this earth and I really believe that.

Looking back, it's wasn't a surprise that when I was asked what I was passionate about at the graduate fair, my response was to get involved in the movement towards the world's peace. I may have been right. I am playing a significant part in bringing peace by applying what Jesus commanded, which is to love my neighbour as myself. Whenever I forgive in my heart or have empathy for the less privileged, I feel inwardly rewarded by God's love. Our love and actions reveal our purpose, without love, there is no purpose in what we do.

1 Corinthians 13: 2-3

2.   If I had the gift of prophecy and knew all about what is going to happen in the future, knew everything about everything, but didn't love others, what good would it do? Even if I had the gift of faith so that I could speak to a mountain and make it move, I would still be worth nothing at all without love.

3.   If I gave everything I have to poor people, and if I were burned alive for preaching the Gospel but didn't love others, it would be of no value whatever."

I have had many more encounters with people I meet every day by showing the love of Christ. It made more sense to me that if the financial sector has been labelled as one of the least reputable sectors then we should expect that some Christians will be assigned to it to transform society. We, therefore shouldn't be surprised when we meet Christians in unusual places, because we are to be planted in every sphere of where God's light is needed.

PURPOSE

During the financial crisis, my boss had observed the way I had engaged with my colleagues and asked how I could be so calm when the economy was so volatile and the future was uncertain. I was a Christian then, not a bold one and my answer could have been more daring and I should probably have said God's calming peace, but I think I may have responded and said quite softly that I had no reason to be frightful.

It is God who delivers and provides us with a safe place. As salt of the earth, we dispense the peace of God to those around us to give them hope. So, love underpins our daily actions, which underpins our values, which underpins our godly purpose.

We can play a part to solve world peace in prominent places such as the United Nations or start by being kind to our neighbours. We would never know how many suicides we have aborted when we've spoken words of hope to dead situations.

Points for Reflection

Our godly purpose to serve others, reveals the nature of God to those who do not yet know Him. It is in Christ, that we discover who we are, for we were formed in God's image. We are His seed, designed for His desire to love the world that He created.

The beautiful exchange of surrendering our lives to God, opens a new path, where we can radiate the Father's love and give selflessly to others.

As we continue to grow to develop a lifestyle of service that glorifies God, He uses us to reach the lost, the broken hearted and those in despair. These acts of kindness draw others to God and they in return, offer up their thanksgiving and praise to our Father. Our purpose brings unity and harmony to help restore a world that is broken and our eternal God is glorified.

Matthew 25:34-40

34. "Then I, the King, shall say to those at my right, 'Come, blessed of my Father, into the Kingdom prepared for you from the founding of the world.

35. For I was hungry and you fed me; I was thirsty and you gave me water; I was a stranger and you invited me into your homes;

36. naked and you clothed me; sick and in prison, and you visited me.'

37. "Then these righteous ones will reply, 'Sir, when did we ever see you hungry and feed you? Or thirsty and give you anything to drink?

38. Or a stranger, and help you? Or naked, and clothe you?

39. When did we ever see you sick or in prison, and visit you?'

40. "And I, the King, will tell them, 'When you did it to these my brothers, you were doing it to me!'"

PURPOSE

Prayer

Dear Lord Jesus,

My confidence is in you.

You alone are my rock and shield.

You protect me all my days.

Help me to fulfil the plans you have for me.

Please open my heart and renew my spirit daily, to see the world through your eyes.

Create in me a passion for your Kingdom.

Grant me the desire to reach the lost.

Make me more willing to obey your commands.

All of this I do, so that I can walk beside you and remain in you.

Your presence is what I crave for, as I live my life out for you.

Amen.

Chapter 6

Building our Character

"And endurance develops strength of character, and character strengthens our confident hope of salvation."

- Romans 5:4

C haracter always involves perseverance. God prepares us adequately for each assignment to enable us to fulfil the plans that He has for us. He is our potter who moulds us for the very purpose for which we were created.

Character isn't a point in time attribution but it is the time difference between two defining periods in our lives. It is the time required for growth through circumstances and events that shape us. How we react during the time between these two periods define our character.

We go through tests and waiting periods to determine what type of foundation we can ultimately rely on in future. The foundation in a house isn't visible to the naked eye but the depth of its structure determines how stable the house stands in horrendous weather. An architect who designs the house will rely on the structure of the building to stand firm for years to come.

In a similar way, these waiting periods require faith, as we do not yet see in the physical the promises we hope for. Therefore, what we do, what we say to others and how we act whilst we wait determines our character. It's as if our character is the invisible core muscle needed to stand firm when the wind blows.

I empathise when I see Christians struggling to stand when they are going through their period of wait and triumph. This is normal; sometimes, we should give permission for what may appear to us as failure for our characters to grow.

Even champions of faith such as Sarah laughed when the Lord promised her a child at the age of ninety. She acted in an uncharacteristic way and lied when confronted, but the Lord still credited her with her faith as she believed that God was able to do what He said He will do.

Genesis 18: 10 - 15

10.   "Then the Lord said, "Next year I will give you and Sarah a son!" (Sarah was listening from the tent door behind him.)

11.   Now Abraham and Sarah were both very old, and Sarah was long since past the time when she could have a baby.

12. So Sarah laughed silently. "A woman my age have a baby?" she scoffed to herself. "And with a husband as old as mine?"

13. Then God said to Abraham, "Why did Sarah laugh? Why did she say 'Can an old woman like me have a baby?'

14. Is anything too hard for God? Next year, just as I told you, I will certainly see to it that Sarah has a son."

15. But Sarah denied it. "I didn't laugh," she lied, for she was afraid.

Hebrews 11:11

"Sarah, too, had faith, and because of this she was able to become a mother in spite of her old age, for she realized that God, who gave her his promise, would certainly do what he said."

I have been here a few times, I have had several cycles of waiting periods and you would think that I should be very good at this now. I am better at waiting but not great at it, I have learnt new things about myself whilst waiting and it is faith that has sustained me.

How have I coped in the waiting room? I did so by sharing my discomfort with my family and close friends. This is because each person is at a different point in the waiting time capsule. Some have seen their promises come through and some are at the early stages, so our stories encourage each other to keep going.

My faith has matured in this process because some of the answers I have seen happen, have not been how I envisioned them to be when I first started praying.

Jeremiah 29:11

"For I know the plans I have for you, says the Lord. They are plans for good and not for disaster, to give you a future and a hope."

I am also more comfortable with God's outcome and that I may not see all my promises on this earth because my true inheritance is being stored for me in eternity. I have learnt to build my character for the entire race and in my daily walk, to fix my eyes on Jesus and enjoy our friendship.

I can rest in any outcome as long as God is with me. That's the only condition I won't compromise on and to be mindful of who I have around encouraging me as I grow my spiritual muscle.

1 Corinthians 15:33

"Do not be misled: "Bad company corrupts good character." "

Developing my character was essential to growing and it involved:
- Testing periods
- Having good people around us
- Recognising that people go through the waiting period at different times

- Answers are not always in the way we expect them
- We rest in Christ knowing His outcome is the best outcome

Our Role Model

"I think a role model is a mentor; someone you see on a daily basis and you learn from them."   - Denzel Washington

Who are our role models? Do we admire them for a particular skill or talent, their physical appearance or do we see a trait in them that we like? Experts say there are three distinct ways we learn and grow: through our actions, by what we see and lastly what we say and hear. Learning through our actions has been shown to be the most impactful way to grow by consciously or subconsciously watching and imitating others.

I tend to watch videos or read biographies on personalities I want to learn something from. This is because I don't have a personal relationship with these individuals and the only access I have is what I can find publicly. Sometimes, I can be a bit direct and I approach those within my reach to ask for their time so I can learn from them and over time, some have evolved to be mentors.

I must say that I have benefitted enormously from having mentors, as they have helped me develop both personally and professionally. However, getting into my mentors' diaries to see them can be very challenging. They have busy lives with competing priorities and their time is carefully managed. If I am lucky, I may get to see my mentor for an hour a month to catch up.

I must say that it is always worth going for my catch ups because in that hour, I get a lot out of them by listening to their experiences and how they have dealt with their challenges. However, time flies quickly and I haven't had the chance to download everything I meant to say. I leave slightly disappointed because I have to wait an entire month for my next catch up session!

Then, I had another light bulb moment, the Holy Spirit speaks to me daily and here, I have no time limit. I realised that I had instant access to a role model that could address all issues in life. Jesus, the Saviour of the world, The Messiah, the one who gave us access to our great God to be co-heirs, is the ultimate role model that was sent to us.

1 John 3:2

"But friends, that's exactly who we are: children of God. And that's only the beginning. Who knows how we'll end up! What we know is that when Christ is openly revealed, we'll see him—and in seeing him, become like him. All of us who look forward to his Coming stay ready, with the glistening purity of Jesus' life as a model for our own."

The good news got better, He has deposited His Spirit within me so I no longer need to rely on imitating others but I can live through Christ and let Him transform me inwardly to build my character.

BUILDING OUR CHARACTER

2 Corinthians 5:17

"Therefore, if anyone is in Christ, he is a new creation; old things have passed away; behold, all things have become new."

I said to myself that since Jesus is the heartbeat of God, He only does what God tells him to do, which then implies that if Christ is in me, and then I too can be the person God created when He formed man in His image. This was a great revelation.

I went back to the Bible and began by studying characters. The characters I came across in the Bible had shared experiences of their weaknesses, their lows, their peaks and triumphs. In addition, they gave a good account of their dependence on God. The Bible has lots of stories that we can learn from and in almost every life situation, I can draw strength from reading great stories of perseverance and hope. Their dependence on God is what sustained them through their trials and it refined their character.

Having access to a daily mentor, Jesus Christ was very refreshing. It is the reason why I set aside time in the morning to learn more and grow in God's character. I found great joy, and suddenly I wanted to tell others. I wanted my friends to share in this revelation of who God is, His nature and for them to receive His blessings - this freedom to live and to be transformed by Him. I too have discovered the (not so) secret lives of Kings and Lords. In fact, my Father sits at the top, as He is the King of Kings and Lord of Lords.

My key lessons:

- Christ is our role model and mentor
- He transforms our lives
- Through the Holy Spirit, we have constant access to God

Romans 12:2

"And do not be conformed to this world [any longer with its superficial values and customs], but be transformed and progressively changed [as you mature spiritually] by the renewing of your mind [focusing on godly values and ethical attitudes], so that you may prove [for yourselves] what the will of God is, that which is good and acceptable and perfect [in His plan and purpose for you]."

Titus 2:7

"... in all things showing yourself to be a pattern of good works; in doctrine showing integrity, reverence, incorruptibility."

God's Grace is for Sons and Daughters (too)

I ventured in my revamped walk with God to tell others about Jesus and the transformation we receive through salvation but there was still a bit of reluctance in me so I asked, "Lord, why wasn't a woman chosen to be one of the main twelve disciples?" It was clear that Jesus had many women who followed Him but it was still a bit unclear to me if we were meant to play a role at the forefront.

This question had played in my subconscious, I don't have the answers to all my questions, however, on reading Romans 16, I saw from Paul's personal greetings to the church that he had commended the women who played a significant role of building the church.

I didn't know the plans God had for me but He provided situations to reveal in part His plans for my life.

I know Jesus absolutely loves me and He wants the best for me, therefore, there is no way He wouldn't give me the best. I stopped making excuses when I felt He was leading me into unknown territories and I allowed Jesus to rebuild my character and in the process, I made the decision every day to do the right thing by pleasing God. Over time, I made better decisions leaning on Christ.

Proverbs 3: 5-6

5. "Trust in the LORD with all your heart and lean not on your own understanding;

6. In all your ways submit to him, and he will make your paths straight."

I loved my grandmother deeply; she was an amazing woman and had a strong character. The meaning of the phrase "to have a strong character", is to be unmoved by outward attractions and stand behind your beliefs. Therefore having a strong character is a good thing if one has godly beliefs and perhaps not so good if we have worldly beliefs.

Matthew 7:21

"Not all who sound religious are really godly people. They may refer to me as 'Lord,' but still won't get to heaven. For the decisive question is whether they obey my Father in heaven."

To describe her, my grandmother was the only child of her mother. Her mother died when she was four months old and she lived independently for most of her life until the age of Ninety-Eight. She was full of wisdom and achieved so much in life despite her early years' setback. She was one of the first female lead broadcasters, after relocating to her home country and fought for women's equality in pay and leadership roles. She told us countless stories of triumph and sowed seeds of great belief in all of us.

I knew she had achieved so much in life but I was unsure whether she had given her life to Christ. Witnessing to family members can seem quite daunting at first especially to those who we assume have everything or are in positions of (worldly) power and influence. We may have looked up to them whilst growing up and now we must tell them that without Christ all is lost.

On what would have been my last visit to her, I asked whilst she was still coherent and could still speak – if she would like to pray and give her life over to Jesus. I held her hand to pray the sinner's prayer of repentance and asked God to forgive her sins. She responded and we were both thankful that she rededicated her life to Christ.

BUILDING OUR CHARACTER

On the day of her funeral, I was filled with God's peace and I knew without a doubt I could stand and say convincingly to our guests that she was a woman of very strong character and Christ was her Saviour.

I had taken a step of faith to evangelise to my grandmother and completed this assignment, I knew God was pleased with me. The Lord knows when we are ready for each task and He continues to mould us by presenting different situations to build our character.

2 Timothy 1:7

"For the Holy Spirit, God's gift, does not want you to be afraid of people, but to be wise and strong, and to love them and enjoy being with them."

The grace to evangelise is available to all men and women. God prepares each of us adequately and He pours out a special anointing for certain tasks so that we can fulfil his plans excellently. It was God's plan to see my grandmother who had achieved so much in her lifetime, be in Heaven with him.

Points for Reflection

We should look to Jesus as our ultimate role model and ask His Holy Spirit to help transform our lives. This special grace, creates a new person in us, the better version of ourselves as God intended.

Building our character takes place in the inner room; it's who we are when no one is watching. We should see our waiting periods as opportunities to live out our faith, trusting that our Father in Heaven desires the best outcome for us.

A godly character that yields from the fruit of the Spirit is to be desired.

Galatians 5:22

"But the fruit of the Spirit is love, joy, peace, forbearance, kindness, goodness, faithfulness, gentleness and self-control."

Prayer

Dear Lord,

Thank you that You continue to challenge me to be a better version of myself.

You desire to see me grow into the very purpose for why I was created.

Thank you for activating my spirit to listen to Your voice to guide me daily.

I see the change already and I must say you have done a good job so far.

I trust Lord that You who began a good work will be faithful to complete Your work in me

I love you.

Chapter 7

Assignments

Date Night

"John replied, "God in heaven appoints each man's work. My work is to prepare the way for that man so that everyone will go to him.

- John 3:27-28

John the Baptist told the crowd that it is God who appoints each man's work and to help others know Jesus. Every day is an opportunity to tell of God's love therefore, my assignment is a daily connection of God's love, loving myself and extending this to those around me.

I had this wonderful opportunity of going to church with my friend who wasn't a Christian. She has always wanted to go to a Christmas Eve service and needed someone to go with her as she wasn't familiar with the order of service. So, I offered to go, was excited and looked forward to it.

Just two days before the special service, I had a traumatic accident. I fell and dislocated my shoulder, describing the pain as excruciating would be an understatement, as the paramedics had to provide a dose of morphine on the spot and then an ambulance came and rushed me to the Emergency Room. Fortunately, the doctors could to reset my shoulder after an hour and I was put in a sling. I was discharged and went back home to rest.

The next day, I was deeply disappointed that I wasn't able to accompany my friend to church. It was strange that even though I had just had the most traumatic experience of physical pain, it was the thought of not going to church that dominated my mind.

In that moment, I had forgotten about my physical condition, rather than pray for healing, I found myself praying to God that I would like to go to church if He would let me. I wanted to share the joy of taking my friend on a special outing, a date with God. And guess what, a miracle happened that night and God filled me with His Power.

I attended the special service and I felt no physical pain. It was an amazing night being in God's Presence and sharing this moment with a close friend. I cried on the inside as God drew me close to him.

Philippians 1:9

"My prayer for you is that you will overflow more and more with love for others and at the same time keep growing in spiritual knowledge and insight".

I knew He had given me divine strength on the day. I certainly understood Paul's words.

Philippians 4:13

"For I can do everything God asks me to with the help of Christ who gives me the strength and power."

I woke up on Christmas day tired and it was God's way of saying now that this assignment is complete, I need you to rest.

The following Sunday, I went to church still recovering and had my shoulder wrapped in a sling. During the worship session, I couldn't lift my hands although my spirit was in full worship. At that moment, My Lord, My God, My Friend said He loved me! The Lord showed me a picture of when Paul was in prison and I said to God, my body may be broken but my spirit is alive and at that moment He filled me with more of His love and of course I cried when I was overwhelmed by the Love I felt for Him. Being filled with the Holy Spirit is the closest bond I ever felt to God, it's an emotion that binds us to Him.

So why do I tell this story? It has some significance to me. I've often wondered why on the two occasions I experienced significant pain, one of which was emotional suffering and the other physical, I had two opposite reactions.

When I experienced emotional suffering from losing a loved one, I moved away from God's presence, I was really hurt and directed my hurt at God. I really love God yet in that situation I was so upset that I chose to close my eyes on God (thankfully, only momentarily). But when I felt extreme physical pain it was the opposite, I pleaded with God that I wanted to reach out, I wanted to be with Him more than ever.

I found that the pain that harms the soul can be more destructive than the pain that harms the body. This is because when the spirit is weak, we may feel more tempted to retreat from God's presence. I learnt whilst reflecting on my experiences that reaching out to those who are suffering on the inside is important, as the greatest temptation to abandoning God or not seeking Him lies in the soul.

Matthew 5: 29-30

29.   "If your right eye causes you to sin, pluck it out and cast it from you; for it is more profitable for you that one of your members perish, than for your whole body to be cast into hell.

30.   And if your right hand causes you to sin, cut it off and cast it from you; for it is more profitable for you that one of your members perish, than for your whole body to be cast into hell..."

Therefore, when we find ourselves weakened by emotional disappointment, the best place to be is in God's presence. Even when we don't feel like it, I want to earnestly say, please find a way to pull through because God always comes through. He doesn't expect us to act or do anything. Just being present and resting in Him is all that is required. When we rest in God's bosom, God is saying,"Don't worry, this time you can just lay low and let me deal with it." He sends messengers to show us His love which helps us to heal and restore our heart.

Romans 8: 35-39

35. "Can anything ever separate us from Christ's love? Does it mean he no longer loves us if we have trouble or calamity, or are persecuted, or hungry, or destitute, or in danger, or threatened with death?

36. (As the Scriptures say, "For your sake we are killed every day; we are being slaughtered like sheep.")

37. No, despite all these things, overwhelming victory is ours through Christ, who loved us.

38. And I am convinced that nothing can ever separate us from God's love. Neither death nor life, neither angels nor demons, neither our fears for today nor our worries about tomorrow—not even the powers of hell can separate us from God's love.

39. No power in the sky above or in the earth below—indeed, nothing in all creation will ever be able to separate us from the love of God that is revealed in Christ Jesus our Lord."

There is a different expectation when we are on God's assignment. His assignment awakens us and it's a time to act. God's assignment is about others, it not about us. We are givers in this season; it allows us to look around to see those need God's help and as God's ambassadors, we are there reaching out and helping others.

God will equip us adequately for His work, more so when we are least qualified to do the job, we only need to get up and move. The Holy Spirit, the same power that was in Christ, is in us now to do the will of the Father.

Partnership

John 4:34-38

34. "Jesus said to them, "My food is to do the will of Him who sent Me, and to finish His work.

35. Do you not say, 'There are still four months and then comes the harvest'? Behold, I say to you, lift up your eyes and look at the fields, for they are already white for harvest!

36. And he who reaps receives wages, and gathers fruit for eternal life, that both he who sows and he who reaps may rejoice together.

37. For in this the saying is true: 'One sows and another reaps.'

38. I sent you to reap that for which you have not laboured; others have laboured, and you have entered into their labours."

Our assignment is a mirror that reflects the image of Christ. We are assigned as messengers to give God's love for someone else to benefit but we shouldn't assume that our messages of hope will be received with open arms.

Sometimes, we may not feel bold enough for the assignment; often due to fear of the resistance that we might face. We may feel comfortable and ask ourselves, why we should invite some sort of disruption to the peace we already have. Likewise, we may be aware of the chaos around us but think it is someone else's job to fix it.

This was the case with Moses when God called him to lead the Israelites out of Egypt. First, he had to confront Pharaoh. Moses' response was that he wasn't the person for the job. God reassured him that he only needed to do as he was told and that He would be with him on his assignment.

Exodus 3:10-15

10. "Now I am going to send you to Pharaoh, to demand that he let you lead my people out of Egypt."

11. But I'm not the person for a job like that!" Moses exclaimed.

12. Then God told him, "I will certainly be with you, and this is the proof that I am the one who is sending you: When you have led the people out of Egypt, you shall worship God here upon this mountain!"

13. But Moses asked, "If I go to the people of Israel and tell them that their fathers' God has sent me, they will ask, 'Which God are you talking about?' What shall I tell them?"

14. 'The Sovereign God,'was the reply. "Just say, 'I Am has sent me!'

15. Yes, tell them, 'Jehovah, the God of your ancestors Abraham, Isaac, and Jacob, has sent me to you.' (This is my eternal name, to be used throughout all generations.)"

FOOTPRINTS OF GRACE

God's sovereignty extends over our lives; it's an eternal promise of who He is. Jesus has given us His spirit to accomplish all things in His name, with an extra dose of boldness that tells us what to say in every situation.

I must say that I have been passive in my Christian walk, and to put it bluntly, I have chosen what I cared about and ignored everything else. I felt that there were mighty men and women more qualified than I to solve the assignments God had for His children, so I couldn't be in the narrative of God's heroes. I knew I was going to go to Heaven – that had been established because I was saved but I thought I didn't have a major role to play. Sometimes, I look back and I'm perplexed about where I got some of my old beliefs from, I was so wrong! We are all heroes in the body of Christ, some are just more active than others.

I shared in the section, Discovering God, the dream I had of the canvas painting, which represented my life being wiped clean and God clearing the clutter to make way for His assignment. Well, a few months after that incident, I was experiencing real growth in my Christian walk, my faith had increased and I believed all things were possible with Christ. The partnership with Christ was going well, and I started to care more about things.

Then one day, God called me a mighty warrior and I thought me? I had heard that the one thing we should be careful asking God is, "Lord, use me". In that one statement, we are committing ourselves to die with Christ, we are prepared to

come out of our comfort zone and do things to push us out to live like Christ. We are prepared to be despised, cursed and suffer for Christ.

Luke 9:23-24

23. "Then he said to all, "Anyone who wants to follow me must put aside his own desires and conveniences and carry his cross with him every day and keep close to me!

24. Whoever loses his life for my sake will save it, but whoever insists on keeping his life will lose it."

There are things I can't explain but when it happened and I heard those words – Mighty Warrior – I had the opposite feeling to fear. I felt courageous; I was finally going to live a life of purpose. Being passive for a few years, sometimes filled with boredom, this new season to move meant that I was finally going to start my very own mini adventure story with God.

Jesus gave me the right partner: The Holy Spirit to go with me.

Gifts and Talents

I have done more for Christ in the last few years than in my passive years of being a Christian. God has blessed me with so many gifts and talents; He has multiplied my abilities for His assignments.

Discovering our gifts and using our talents is our service to the Lord. God expects us to excel with the talent He has given us.

He expects us to give our best. Jesus told the story of the parable of the talents to illustrate that for the servant who did nothing, his talent will be taken away and given to the one who returned a ten-fold increase.

Matthew 25:28-29

28. "Then he ordered, 'Take the money from this servant, and give it to the one with the ten bags of silver.

29. To those who use well what they are given, even more will be given, and they will have an abundance. But from those who do nothing, even what little they have will be taken away."

I asked myself what I was most passionate about that I could use to serve? I wanted to find out what I could do that would bring me joy. This question helped me to examine the things I enjoyed doing almost effortlessly or where I felt highly rewarded when the tasks were completed.

To my surprise, I found out that the one thing I really enjoyed was meeting people and forming relationships. I love hosting people at home and I also enjoy going out. Though I realised over time that I couldn't have the depth of relationship I would have liked with most people and so I settled with a few close relationships but connected with most people.

In our gatherings, I enjoy stories that make me erupt in laughter. Happiness and laughter are infectious. My grandmother was a radio personality and she knew how to tell the most outrageous stories that got us rolling on the floor. I learnt from her, I developed my version of narrating events and love making people laugh. With an outgoing personality and being a chatter box, God took all of me for His work.

But first He had work to do. I had to pick up new gifts and abilities.

Here are two real examples of how I feel God has multiplied my abilities.

I will start by explaining briefly where I started from. I was working in the City of London and attended church regularly on Sundays. After my revived encounter with God, I took the first step to volunteer at Church. I like welcoming people and so I joined the hosting team. It was nice to connect with regular members, asking about their week and it fitted nicely with my routine.

After several months of hosting, one day, I received what seemed like a random invite to attend a Home Group Leader's training course. We never planned to have a home group, it certainly wasn't on our radar of the things we thought we were ready for. However, my husband and I thought we had a bit of time and we should go to learn something new, and off we went.

It was an interesting course, we learnt about how to run a small diverse group and facilitate discussions but it took 18 months from when we completed the training to when we made a commitment to eventually start one. It was a long-term commitment which we carefully thought about and it's been a great blessing since we made the decision to start. I enjoy hosting our group, we have a meal together, get to talk about our week and it's great to see a mini community that supports each other.

We have since had a few more surprising phone calls encouraging us to attend the prayer ministry course - learning how to pray for people and the one that got me rolling, was attending a preaching course. It is still mind boggling to see bankers attending a course on how to preach about the love of Christ. I felt I could talk about Christ as that was perhaps easy but preaching was for vicars.

We went ahead and to our delight it was such a useful course as it helped to hone in on our communication skills and how to engage with an audience, which is a far greater skill that applies to every works of life. I am now using these skills I have learnt in multiple areas of my life.

Does this apply at work too? I can say absolutely yes. I had the amazing opportunity of attending a Leadership Conference. Its slogan was 'For Leaders, For Learners, For those that will make a difference.' I didn't consider myself a leader, I wasn't running a major company I thought, but I was a learner and certainly curious, so I signed up for it. I think the Holy Spirit must have also prompted me.

ASSIGNMENTS

The speakers had amazing insights on leadership, one thing I took away was that change happens at all levels and even if you can't influence at the top you can influence those around you. I went back to work reinvigorated and became more aware of my surrounding. I started speaking up, asking questions, I became bolder in meetings, providing ideas – silly ones that no one dared to ask.

I moved around within the company and in a short space of time I had acquired many skills. I also developed more of an interest in broader topics such as diversity and ethnic minority issues in the work place, graduate mentoring, family network. I volunteered my time and got involved because I started caring.

One day I got yet another random call to attend a think-tank event in the Financial City of London, providing ideas to solve ethical and social issues. I had grown professionally over time and expanded my skills in the process. My activities went beyond my job description and I felt fulfilled and enjoyed going to work.

In the process, I met a few people who I engaged with and I shared my journey with them. Things have evolved, my husband and I now mentor youths, those who need some career advice and somehow, we have become useful in helping others.

In small groups, I also tell people of my adventure stories, these are personal stories, real stories of God's victory in my life. I tell my stories to make people laugh, lift them up and if one person in the room leaves feeling encouraged, I know God is at work.

Allowing Jesus to direct our path, when the Holy Spirit nudges us to attend random meetings, courses, events or conferences to submit. These are subtle ways we can acquire new talents and insights to grow.

When I look back at the opportunities I have had, I can say God isn't random at all. He opens new doors to prepare us for new opportunities. These opportunities allow us to use our talents to be impactful to those around us as we care about what matters to God.

I have rebranded myself as a seed planter, sowing seeds of joy and hope, knowing someone will water the soil and someone will be there at harvest time. There is a time and a place for each person to find God's love and to also give God's love. It's never too late to start.

A Time for Everything

Ecclesiastes 3
1.   "For everything there is a season,
        A time for every activity under heaven.
2.   A time to be born and a time to die.
        A time to plant and a time to harvest.

ASSIGNMENTS

3.　　A time to kill and a time to heal.

　　　A time to tear down and a time to build up.

4.　　A time to cry and a time to laugh.

　　　A time to grieve and a time to dance.

5.　　A time to scatter stones and a time to gather stones.

　　　A time to embrace and a time to turn away.

6.　　A time to search and a time to quit searching.

　　　A time to keep and a time to throw away.

7.　　A time to tear and a time to mend.

　　　A time to be quiet and a time to speak.

8.　　A time to love and a time to hate.

　　　A time for war and a time for peace.

9.　　What do people really get for all their hard work?

10.　　I have seen the burden God has placed on us all.

11.　　Yet God has made everything beautiful for its own time. He has planted eternity in the human heart, but even so, people cannot see the whole scope of God's work from beginning to end.

12.　　So I concluded there is nothing better than to be happy and enjoy ourselves as long as we can.

13.　　And people should eat and drink and enjoy the fruits of their labour, for these are gifts from God.

14.　　And I know that whatever God does is final. Nothing can be added to it or taken from it. God's purpose is that people should fear him.

Points for Reflection

We should believe that God is a giver of good gifts and his timing is perfect. Our father watches over us and wants us to grow into our destiny. In His infinite wisdom, He doesn't give us more than we can bear but instead creates opportunities to strengthen our faith to believe all things are possible with Him.

We should tune our ears to hear God clearly; His ways are not random at all. Therefore, at every opportunity when we see doors open (the right door may I add), we should trust God that he has made the right provisions available to enable us to succeed.

God's gift to us and our use of it, makes His glory shine even more. We are God's testimony to those that don't know Him yet.

James 1: 17-18

17.   "Whatever is good and perfect is a gift coming down to us from God our Father, who created all the lights in the heavens. He never changes or casts a shifting shadow.

18.   He chose to give birth to us by giving us his true word. And we, out of all creation, became his prized possession."

ASSIGNMENTS

Prayer of Victory and Thanksgiving

Almighty God, I thank You for everything You have done for me; my salvation, Your grace, Your love and Your protection.

I thank You for today and the gift to call You Abba Father. I come to You for my daily bread where there is Life! Lord today, I carry my cross to follow You. I'll follow You all the days of my life.

You choose from the humblest background to do great things. For You breathe Your Spirit upon us to show Your power. You do great things for You are great, Your name is great. Your power equips us for the work You have for us.

You called us to love and You give us the ability to love so we can carry out Your plans with a sincere heart.

Lord, You anointed Saul to be king, a Benjamite from the least tribe of Israel. But You were unhappy with Israel for wanting a king and You hardened Saul's heart to oppress the people of Israel.

But Your love bursts forth again! What amazing love, for who can know Your ways. You anointed David as king and chose a man after Your own heart. The least of his brothers but You made him great.

You always look at our heart and never the outward appearance. Even when we sin and come back repenting; You embrace us. I am sorry for the things I have done to You. Jesus, my sins drove You to the cross, but Your love came down to rescue me.

Amazing grace. You have restored me and provided a crown over my household.

For it is this faith that brings true deliverance and heavenly rewards.

Thank you for the victory that has been won to make me Yours forever.

Part III

Part III

Chapter 8

Impacting Others

Loving Others as Ourselves

"Let me give you a new command: Love one another. In the same way I loved you, you love one another. This is how everyone will recognize that you are my disciples—when they see the love you have for each other."

- John 13: 34-35

I love the gathering of God's people and I'm quite joyful when I'm around loved ones. This family "our brothers and sisters" are a gift from God; they rejoice with us when we celebrate and are there for us when we are down.

I mentioned in the last chapter that we lead a small house group fellowship. It's a way for us to stay connected with friends. I enjoy the discussions we have, our stories of God and our common love for Christ. I love that each one of us has an individual story of God's grace to share. It is amazing because it allows me to see another facet of God, through their different experiences of how they relate to God. That's because we are very different in the way we express ourselves.

I call them "friends" but would I have previously chosen them into my close-knit group? No. I thought we didn't have anything in common but Christ. I saw no semblance in our interests or in what I was passionate about. However, when I realised that I was deeply passionate about Christ, I became attracted to Him in others.

Matthew 5:16

"Don't hide your light! Let it shine for all; let your good deeds glow for all to see, so that they will praise your heavenly Father."

Without the lens of Christ, our differences are exaggerated and we can become slightly disillusioned, allowing disunity to slowly creep in. At Christian events, I expect attendees to be well behaved and get upset if people act otherwise, for instance, in an event when we had to queue up for meals and the queues became rowdy.

I also noticed that some Christians are more generous in general matters and some seem to have more compassion on specific issues. These differences can be slightly confusing to a bystander because each one campaigns for its own cause. It was only much later that I realised that God expected all of us to have some measure of all the fruits of the spirit and He intended for all of us to live in harmony with our differences.

1 Corinthians 12: 22-26

22.   "In fact, some parts of the body that seem weakest and least important are actually the most necessary.

23.   And the parts we regard as less honourable are those we clothe with the greatest care. So we carefully protect those parts that should not be seen,

24.   while the more honourable parts do not require this special care. So God has put the body together such that extra honour and care are given to those parts that have less dignity.

25.   This makes for harmony among the members, so that all the members care for each other.

26.   If one part suffers, all the parts suffer with it, and if one part is honoured, all the parts are glad."

It didn't matter that we were different, what mattered was that the Holy Spirit transforms us to produce the fruits of God's Kingdom.

Galatians 5:22-23

"But the Holy Spirit produces this kind of fruit in our lives: love, joy, peace, patience, kindness, goodness, faithfulness, gentleness, and self-control. There is no law against these things!"

My perspective changed after being filled with an extra dose of God's love. I asked the Holy Spirit to open my heart to teach me how to relate and love my brothers and sisters from such diverse backgrounds.

The Holy Spirit explained that every Christian has the blood of Christ flowing through them. However, just like our body parts, the quantity of blood needed for the brain is very different to the quantity needed for the eyes or feet, but it is the same blood and one body.

Romans 12:4-5

4   "For just as each of us has one body with many members, and these members do not all have the same function,

5.   So in Christ we, though many, form one body, and each member belongs to all the others."

During my transformation period (this is still ongoing), I had to renew my mind and Jesus became the defender of my mind craft games. Each time I wanted to criticise someone, I saw Jesus all over them and of course that melted my heart and I couldn't say a word. My thoughts towards that person changed to love and I realised that my heart had softened over time. However, I was partial towards Christians behaving badly and I forgave them easily just as I would towards my little sister.

My convictions got worse, at the office; I had some challenges with some of my colleagues. We didn't seem to be on the same page on work issues. I reacted as Christians would and bore the brunt of not confronting the issues since we were meant to be long suffering but I knew that I still had unsettling thoughts of resentment.

What happened next was something I could not have predicted. I didn't expect my workplace to have a Christian fellowship, so I was pleasantly surprised when I heard there was a lunch time Christian Bible study group and decided to go.

On my way to the Bible study group, I left my work station and saw one of my said colleagues in the lift and chatted a bit. When Igot out, of the lift I thought it was time to part ways and she'll go off to get her lunch. However, she kept walking in the same direction and at one point, I thought she was going to another meeting, possibly next door to where mine was taking place, but she continued until we ended up at the same Bible study group. She sat next to me and it was a Holy Spirit 'gotcha' moment. I learnt a lesson to be more patient in my dealings with others and to always see Christ in every person.

The more I saw Christ in a person, the more I could love them and this radically changed my interactions with Christians and non-Christians. It wasn't my place to judge rather it is my place to love in a non-judgmental way.

I must confess that I still show favouritism to my brothers and sisters in Christ, as the saying, "blood is thicker than water" reminds us that our family relationships are more important. So, you can still tell I have a long way to go reaching the standards Jesus sets for us, telling us to love our enemies. I am just about there, getting to love my family, the Body of Christ as myself.

Matthew 5: 43-48

Love for Enemies

43. "You have heard that it was said, 'Love your neighbour and hate your enemy.'

44. But I tell you, love your enemies and pray for those who persecute you,

45 that you may be children of your Father in heaven. He causes his sun to rise on the evil and the good, and sends rain on the righteous and the unrighteous.

46. If you love those who love you, what reward will you get? Are not even the tax collectors doing that?

47. And if you greet only your own people, what are you doing more than others? Do not even pagans do that?

48. Be perfect, therefore, as your heavenly Father is perfect."

Body of Christ

Acts 2:44-46

44. "And all the believers met together constantly and shared everything with each other,

45. selling their possessions and dividing with those in need.

46. They worshiped together regularly at the Temple each day, met in small groups in homes for Communion, and shared their meals with great joy and thankfulness,

47. Praising God."

Serving others has been a virtue I was accustomed to, growing up. I come from a culture where our community was responsible for raising the children in the local neighbourhood. My extended family played as much of an important role as my nuclear family did, on family matters. When we had family functions, my aunties, uncles and cousins gathered round to divide the tasks as required.

In addition, they all contributed into a joint pot of money to support each other financially whenever there was a large occasion, to ease the burden for the main organiser. I witnessed communal joy and happiness amongst my relatives.

However, I was deeply moved when I saw this bond exist outside of blood relatives, especially in moments of despair, when individuals who were unrelated gave the same amount of contribution and affection to one another. I saw the depth of God's love as I understood that the grace of God extended to cover His Kingdom family and God was the true source of compassion.

Jesus extended our family relationships to include the Body of Christ, our brothers and sisters who follow God and do His will. This extended family is a gift from God allowing more access to our Father in Heaven.

Mark 3: 33-35

33.   "But He answered them, saying, "Who is My mother, or My brothers?"

FOOTPRINTS OF GRACE

34.   And He looked around in a circle at those who sat about Him, and said, "Here are My mother and My brothers!

35.   For whoever does the will of God is My brother and My sister and mother."

Everyone in this adopted family has the spirit of God, more so special gifts to dispense the love of God to others. Jesus said, in John 13:34-35, "And so I am giving a new commandment to you now—love each other just as much as I love you.[35] Your strong love for each other will prove to the world that you are my disciples."

Therefore, as disciples bearing the witness of God's grace, our lives reflect Christ like characters so that our interaction with our brothers and sisters should allow us to experience God when we live a life of serving others. This is where we expect charity and love to begin, a safe place to be ourselves, with unconditional love and open arms, for without God it is impossible to love. John says it slightly different in 1 John 4:8 - He who does not love does not know God, for God is love.

The indwelling of the Holy Spirit unifies the Body of Christ. We are the temple of God, a safe tower where we collectively meet to embrace one another with God's affection. It has been amazing to see each person warmly accepted and encouraged to keep growing in their faith at our small groups. Therefore, as we walk together, cheering each other on, we experience the glory of God in our gatherings.

IMPACTING OTHERS

John 17:22-23

22.   And the glory which You gave Me I have given them,
        that they may be one just as We are one:

23.   I in them, and You in Me; that they may be made perfect
        in one, and that the world may know that You have sent
        Me, and have loved them as You have loved Me."

As Christ lives in us, it becomes easier to also carry each
other's burdens. The Holy Spirit fills us with the power to
accomplish good deeds and our assignments become more
apparent when we are moved by grace to help the Body of
Christ, our family, in times of need. I tell friends not to fret
during their testing periods because our help comes from God
in unexpected places and unrelated persons.

God's Steward
Our obedience is someone else's miracle.

David addressed the people when he commissioned the
building of the temple.

1 Chronicles 29: 3 - 5

3.   "And now, because of my devotion to the Temple of
        God, I am giving all of my own private treasures to aid in
        the construction. This is in addition to the building
        materials I have already collected.

4-5.   These personal contributions consist of millions of
        dollars of gold from Ophir and huge amounts of silver to

be used for overlaying the walls of the buildings. It will also be used for the articles made of gold and silver and for the artistic decorations. Now then, who will follow my example? Who will give himself and all that he has to the Lord?"

The cry of David in first Chronicles still resonates with us today. Everything we own comes from God and it is by the grace of God that we can abound in all things. Therefore, we are now building God's temple – His Church and we've all been called to participate in giving to His Kingdom.

The gift of life, our labour and our accompanying success has been bestowed upon us by God, the provider of all things. Our Father delights to give us the desires of our heart, and His generosity is stewarded through others. Our giving to others activates the charitable heart of the Father and it draws us closer to Him.

Whenever I acted under my own abilities to accomplish anything, I found that I was striving rather than excelling in what I did. I put in twice the effort, which was time consuming and I expended loads of energy. But when I became fully dependent on God, and did not worry so much, God opened doors for me to excel in what I did and I enjoyed the fruits of my labour. Now, I do most things with joy and it makes me feel close to the Father. With this partnership, I have a great bond and I'm free to live, free to give and free to love.

Here is another way to put it: God's generosity towards us is a seed, which flourishes as we give of ourselves to others. The parable of the talent brings to bear, as we can multiply that which was sown in us. Therefore, we evolve over time from being receivers of God's blessings to also givers of His blessings. We become His vessels meeting the needs of those around us.

2 Corinthians 9:6

"Now [remember] this: he who sows sparingly will also reap sparingly, and he who sows generously [that blessings may come to others] will also reap generously [and be blessed]."

The blessings that come to those that give, applies to all, however Christians who do not give short-change themselves when it rains from Heaven. The Bible says that those who sow sparingly reap sparingly and the opposite is true that our giving opens favour from other men which increases our harvest. Let's imagine that each time we make ourselves available, we open ourselves to more opportunities.

I listened to one of Andrew Wommack's talks on Financial Stewardship, where he explained the favour we can expect from man with the parable of the shrewd accountant. The shrewd accountant used the resources given to him to manage, for his benefit by granting his master's debtors a discount, so he could obtain favours from them after losing his job.

Luke 16: 8 – 12

8.   "The master commended the dishonest manager because he had acted shrewdly. For the people of this world are more shrewd in dealing with their own kind than are the people of the light.

9.   I tell you, use worldly wealth to gain friends for yourselves, so that when it is gone, you will be welcomed into eternal dwellings.

10.   "Whoever can be trusted with very little can also be trusted with much, and whoever is dishonest with very little will also be dishonest with much.

11.   So if you have not been trustworthy in handling worldly wealth, who will trust you with true riches?

12.   And if you have not been trustworthy with someone else's property, who will give you property of your own?

Non-Christians understand the blessings that come from being charitable, sometimes, more than Christians. Jesus used this parable to illustrate that people who belong to this world are cleverer in dealing with their peers than people who belong to the light.

What I took away from his talk was that we are custodians of God's resources; we are not expected to waste what He has given us to manage but to use these to gain favour as we bless others.

Our obedience as God instructs us to release His blessing to others becomes the answer to prayers for those praying for a miracle. It's a circle of grace by which God has promised to those who are faithful that we should not lack in anything when we submit to the will of God.

Acts 2:42-47

42. "All the believers devoted themselves to the apostles' teaching, and to fellowship, and to sharing in meals (including the Lord's Supper), and to prayer.

43. A deep sense of awe came over them all, and the apostles performed many miraculous signs and wonders.

44. And all the believers met together in one place and shared everything they had.

45. They sold their property and possessions and shared the money with those in need.

46. They worshiped together at the Temple each day, met in homes for the Lord's Supper, and shared their meals with great joy and generosity—

47. All the while praising God and enjoying the goodwill of all the people. And each day the Lord added to their fellowship those who were being saved."

Blessed to Be a Blessing

Partnership with the Holy Spirit is essential to bearing God's fruits. The Lord knows the needs of every person and being sensitive allows us to cooperate better in our labouring of love to others. Discerning the will of God makes our act of giving more effective. This is because we often get it wrong when we are moved by outside appearances and we misjudge.

As an example, I was led to put some money into a friend's account and trust God that it was the right thing to do. My friend was surprised because I was unaware of his challenges but this act of kindness touched him. He called later that day to thank me and prayed for me.

The following day, I was travelling with one of my best friends to celebrate a milestone birthday of another close friend. I was quite tired, I'd had a hectic month at work, wasn't sleeping well and I really needed a holiday to unwind and rest. We planned and met at the airport to connect and board the flight.

When I got to the airport to check in, I realised that my friend had upgraded our tickets. I remembered the conversations I had with God a few times that week that I was physically tired and needed a good rest. I told my friend that her (Spirit led) act of kindness had touched me; her kindness reminded me that Jesus cared for me, He was interested in every detail of my life and nothing was too small to ignore. I thanked her and throughout the duration of the flight, I rested in God's love and thanked Him.

When we touch the lives of others particularly when it is God led, the experience can be very powerful because it draws that individual into God's love. It causes others (the receiver) to bless God and raises their level of intimacy with God.

I'd like to encourage Christians to give with a cheerful heart and to be led by the Holy Spirit to give in the most effective way, starting with where we receive the Word of God, our church, so that we can partake in the harvest and receive more people into God's Kingdom.

2 Corinthians 9: 5 – 15

5.   "So I have asked these other brothers to arrive ahead of me to see that the gift you promised is on hand and waiting. I want it to be a real gift and not look as if it were being given under pressure.

6.   But remember this—if you give little, you will get little. A farmer who plants just a few seeds will get only a small crop, but if he plants much, he will reap much.

7.   Everyone must make up his own mind as to how much he should give. Don't force anyone to give more than he really wants to, for cheerful givers are the ones God prizes.

8.   God is able to make it up to you by giving you everything you need and more so that there will not only be enough for your own needs but plenty left over to give joyfully to others.

9.   It is as the Scriptures say: "The godly man gives generously to the poor. His good deeds will be an honour to him forever."

10. For God, who gives seed to the farmer to plant, and later on good crops to harvest and eat, will give you more and more seed to plant and will make it grow so that you can give away more and more fruit from your harvest.

11. Yes, God will give you much so that you can give away much, and when we take your gifts to those who need

them they will break out into thanksgiving and praise to God for your help.

12. So two good things happen as a result of your gifts—those in need are helped, and they overflow with thanks to God.

13. Those you help will be glad not only because of your generous gifts to themselves and to others, but they will praise God for this proof that your deeds are as good as your doctrine.

14. And they will pray for you with deep fervour and feeling because of the wonderful grace of God shown through you.

15, Thank God for his Son—his Gift too wonderful for words."

Points for Reflection

We should live for Christ and radiate His love to our neighbours and friends through our daily actions.

God longs for us to have enriching lives.

The blessing of the Lord makes a person rich, and he adds no sorrow with it (Proverbs 10:22). However, the perfect debt is our acts of love to others.

"Owe no one anything except to love one another, for he who loves another has fulfilled the law". Romans 13:8

IMPACTING OTHERS

Our Father in Heaven, is a good God, His infinite and boundless nature means He is more than able to replenish our resources, so that we can continue to flourish.

We should seek to do those simple acts of service that bring a smile to our faces, because true joy transforms us and lifts us to a higher platform of everlasting peace, by rewarding us with a richness in our spirit.

Let's ask ourselves, how can we express our worship to God by loving others? Are we living as salt of the earth? Do we find ourselves striving in the gifts God has blessed us with?

My Prayer of Covenant

Dear God,

You are a covenant keeping God

You speak to us in such a loving way

We are learning to trust and obey Your commands

We don't know tomorrow but we know You

Father it's been our delight to know that we don't have to worry about anything

Father You said You like our obedience and it's been a delight to watch us grow

Help us to balance the commitments we have, to give whole-heartedly and above all to live generously.

Help us to be disciplined with the resources You have given us; For You said You would bless us abundantly.

Lord, may Your church be blessed and may we continue to enjoy the fellowship of the Body of Christ.

May we overflow with genuine love for each other.

Thank You Lord for everything.

Amen.

Final words......

Part IV

Part IV

Chapter 9

Lasting Dynasty

NextGen

"That is why he is the one who mediates a new covenant between God and people, so that all who are called can receive the eternal inheritance God has promised them. For Christ died to set them free from the penalty of the sins they had committed under that first covenant."

- Hebrews 9:15

Some leave behind worldly possessions; others go an extra mile to leave their legacy but our Saviour Jesus Christ left us with an eternal inheritance. As co-heirs to the Kingdom of God, we share in this heavenly promise.

I read the book of Judges and imagined Joshua leading Israel to the Promise Land with songs of praise. The journey to the Promise Land was a great triumph. The people saw the dramatic hand of God as He delivered them from Pharaoh. There was unity amongst all tribes and they worshipped God with all their heart.

The story proceeded to show what happens when generations move away from God's presence, abandoning their faith in God and following idols. They consequently moved away from the presence of God and sadly, it ended with the tribe of Benjamin going into battle with their brothers. The people God united were now at war with each other; it was recorded that everyone did as they liked.

Judges 21: 6

"6 Now the Israelites grieved for the tribe of Benjamin, their fellow Israelites. "Today one tribe is cut off from Israel," they said."

Judges 21: 25

"25 In those days Israel had no king; everyone did as they saw fit."

The absence of God brings disharmony. Without God, there is no peace. There are families in court today, disputing their inheritances and creating disunity amongst themselves. It is sad to see such happen because whilst the Bible says that it is good for parents to leave worldly possessions for their offspring, Christ came and gave us much more.

Proverbs 13:22.

"When a good man dies, he leaves an inheritance to his grandchildren."

LASTING DYNASTY

Acts 20:32

"And now I entrust you to God and his care and to his wonderful words that are able to build your faith and give you all the inheritance of those who are set apart for himself."

Sadly, I think there are some children who doubt themselves and do not believe that they can surpass their parent's legacy and so, they are afraid to step out into the big world. David understood the fear a child could have of being intimidated by very successful parents, so he prayed for his son Solomon in 1 Chronicles 29:19 – "Give my son Solomon a good heart towards God, so that he will want to obey you in the smallest details and will look forward eagerly to finishing the building of your temple for which I have made all of these preparations.".

As a parent, I am reminded often whether I have done enough to prepare a foundation in my children's spiritual lives so that they too can develop their faith to believe in God Almighty, the giver of all, who enables us to excel in all things.

I pray constantly for them and teach about my faith to equip them with a strong foundation in Christ. This is the inheritance I want to leave, the "Spirit of God", to plant Christ's seed in their hearts so that it may grow years after we have left this world. For I know that we pass on a light that can never be quenched nor destroyed; instead, it provides eternal life. What joy it would be to see our children in eternity knowing that they too completed their race.

I tell my children to pray everyday, I want them to know that when the fear of failure looms, they know to dismiss it because that's not the inheritance given to them. I want to teach them to have courage like Elisha, to ask for a double portion of the love and protection that God gave to their parents.

I pray also for my grandchildren, that they too may in their time, ask for a double portion of God's provision given to their parents. For if each generation were to ask for a double portion of God's grace, the world will see a shift to holiness.

2 Kings 2:9

"9 When they arrived on the other side Elijah said to Elisha, "What wish shall I grant you before I am taken away?" And Elisha replied, "Please grant me twice as much prophetic power as you have had.""

Finishing the Race

"The desires of the diligent are fully satisfied."

Proverbs 13:4

The Lord knows who we are; He knows us by name and calls us to our own personal goals. If we run our own race and focus on our lane, then we are more likely to reach the end. What counts at the end of our race is that we reach the finishing line.

Imitating others, even our role models, can be a limiting factor. Instead, we should strive to be the best of ourselves knowing our character is formed in Christ. We must be authentic in our obedience and walk with God because doubt often comes when we compare ourselves to others especially when we seem to be failing terribly at it.

We should never worry about being different for God, we are all connected by one Spirit and there is unity in the Body of Christ. The Bible says in Ephesians 4 to make every effort to keep yourselves united in the Spirit, binding yourselves together with peace. For there is one body and one Spirit, just as you have been called to one glorious hope for the future.

Often, I get asked, how do I pray? How did I grow in my faith? I tell them I sought God's face earnestly and He enveloped me in His arms. Though, this wasn't how I started my journey, I was insecure in my faith and didn't expect the blessings that I now enjoy. I relied on my own strength and ability and whenever the Lord asked me to take a step of faith on an assignment, I compared myself to others.

I gave several reasons why I couldn't take on an assignment and made excuses that I wasn't the best person for the job. They appeared quite challenging and I let fear creep in. I learnt with time that God won't give us an assignment for us to fail. Even when it's stretching, He gives us signs through our 'Red Sea' moments to trust Him. Our trust in God turns our fears into hope, because He doesn't expect us to do them in our own strength. He sends the Holy Spirit to partner with us and shows us great signs and wonders to help us take a leap of faith.

He provided signs to Moses to show that it was He who was sending him. When these miracles happen in our lives, we should know it's time to act and we will succeed.

God meets us where we are and at the right time, He asks us to take a step further and trust in Him. This often happens during the strengthening period and we see the miracles come forth. So, when God asks us to step out in a way that exceeds our expectations, we should shut the door quietly and let God lead. He tells us not to be afraid. However, we must tune our ears to God, because we only hear Him if we listen.

I had to learn the art of listening to God by being still and resting in His presence. He talks to all of us in very different ways so you must ask God to show you the language that connects with your own spirit. My best times are first thing in the morning and the last thing at night, meditating on how great and good God is.

The Psalmist says in Psalm 1:2, "But they delight in doing everything God wants them to, and day and night are always meditating on his laws and thinking about ways to follow him more closely."

I'm astonished at how peaceful it is to lie down in the presence of God, resting and growing in the intimate knowledge of knowing Him. It is a delight to worship God in Spirit and have Him respond with His wonderful words.

This is what God intended when He created the universe, that we would be in constant fellowship with Him, enjoying the beauty of the earth. I look out and see trees, the sky and moon gazing down and these are truly marvellous creations.

I know what it means to know God and indeed those with their inheritance secured in Heaven are the ones who indeed have everything. I am at peace and I can boldly say I have everything through Christ Jesus.

A Note to My Children

I am not a writer, nor a preacher; I'm just mum passing on the source of my faith. When I leave this earth, I pray you have a double portion of what the Lord has given us. Hold the Bible daily in your hands, imprint God's ways in your heart and have this book as a symbol of your "stone" of faith.

We modelled the life of Jesus and accepted Him as our Lord and Saviour. We followed His commandment to love God and love others.

Matthew 22: 37-40

37.   "Jesus replied, "'You must love the Lord your God with all your heart, all your soul, and all your mind.'

38.   This is the first and greatest commandment.

39.   A second is equally important: 'Love your neighbour as yourself.'

40.   The entire law and all the demands of the prophets are based on these two commandments."

It all starts and ends with God (Love) for God is Love. It starts in the heart. Learn to love, obey and follow Christ always. Work hard to achieve excellence in whatever you do. Live a life of purpose following God's path; when you have learnt and understood God's promises and purpose for your life, write down your stories, and teach your children too.

Your parents are passing their inheritance to you. If you accept Jesus as your Saviour, you will have a lasting dynasty that outlasts generations.

Psalm 22:30

"Our children will also serve him. Future generations will hear about the wonders of the Lord."

Points for Reflection

Must I Go, and Empty Handed?

Gospel Hymns No.3 1878

Charles Luther (1847-1924) was a journalist who later became an ordained Baptist Minister in 1886. He wrote the hymn, "Must I Go, And Empty Handed" after he'd heard the story of a young man who was about to die. He'd only been a Christian for a month; he was regreftful because he had very little opportunity to serve the Lord. The young boy was quoted to have said "I am not afraid to die; Jesus saves me now. But must I go empty handed?".

This Hymn highlights the urgency of embracing a godly purpose to use the gifts that God has given us, to serve others and also lead them to Christ.

Similarly, I recently read an article, which suggested that it was written by Steve Jobs, the Apple founder on his deathbed. However, whilst the legitimacy of this note has been challenged, the words written express the regrets many people face when they chase material dreams and in the process, ignore fruitful personal relationships.

Copies of both the Hymn and Article are in the appendix.

All of us must quickly carry out the tasks assigned us by the one who sent me, for there is little time left before the night falls and all work comes to an end. John 9:4

Final Prayer – Jesus Christ Our Lord and Saviour

I would like to finish this book with a prayer that changed my life, the prayer of our Lord Jesus prayed at His final hours on earth for all those who believe in him. It's our assurance that death is not the end and that we will pass on in glory to join our Father in Heaven. How marvellous will it be to see Him in His full glory! This is the foundation of our Faith that Jesus came to die for us so we can have an eternal life.

John 17

Jesus Prays to Be Glorified

17. "After Jesus said this, he looked toward heaven and prayed:

1. "Father, the hour has come. Glorify your Son, that your Son may glorify you.

2. For you granted him authority over all people that he might give eternal life to all those you have given him.

3. Now this is eternal life: that they know you, the only true God, and Jesus Christ, whom you have sent.

4. I have brought you glory on earth by finishing the work you gave me to do. 5. And now, Father, glorify me in your presence with the glory I had with you before the world began.

5. Jesus Prays for His Disciples

6. I have revealed you to those whom you gave me out of the world. They were yours; you gave them to me and they have obeyed your word.

7.   Now they know that everything you have given me comes from you.

8.   For I gave them the words you gave me and they accepted them. They knew with certainty that I came from you, and they believed that you sent me.

9.   I pray for them. I am not praying for the world, but for those you have given me, for they are yours.

10.   All I have is yours, and all you have is mine. And glory has come to me through them.

11.   I will remain in the world no longer, but they are still in the world, and I am coming to you. Holy Father, protect them by the power of] your name, the name you gave me, so that they may be one as we are one.

12.   While I was with them, I protected them and kept them safe by that name you gave me. None has been lost except the one doomed to destruction so that Scripture would be fulfilled.

13.   "I am coming to you now, but I say these things while I am still in the world, so that they may have the full measure of my joy within them.

14.   I have given them your word and the world has hated them, for they are not of the world any more than I am of the world.

15.   My prayer is not that you take them out of the world but that you protect them from the evil one.

16.   They are not of the world, even as I am not of it.

17.   Sanctify them by the truth; your word is truth.

18.   As you sent me into the world, I have sent them into the world.

19.   For them I sanctify myself, that they too may be truly sanctified.

Jesus Prays for All Believers

20.   "My prayer is not for them alone. I pray also for those who will believe in me through their message,

21.   That all of them may be one, Father, just as you are in me and I am in you. May they also be in us so that the world may believe that you have sent me.

22.   I have given them the glory that you gave me, that they may be one as we are one—

23.   I in them and you in me—so that they may be brought to complete unity. Then the world will know that you sent me and have loved them even as you have loved me.

24.   "Father, I want those you have given me to be with me where I am, and to see my glory, the glory you have given me because you loved me before the creation of the world.

25.   "Righteous Father, though the world does not know you, I know you, and they know that you have sent me.

26.   I have made you known to them, and will continue to make you known in order that the love you have for me may be in them and that I myself may be in them."

APPENDIX I

References: Bible Passages

PART 1	PART 1
CHAPTER 1	**CHAPTER 1**
Joshua 4: 21-24	NLT
Genesis 1: 27-28	NIV
Genesis 2: 8-9, 15-17	NLT
Genesis 3: 22-23	NIV
John 3: 16-17	NLT
Hebrews 11: 1-3	NLT
Hebrews 8:11	NIV
Proverbs 8: 30-32	NIV
Romans 5: 6-8	NIV
1 John 4:19	NIV
Proverbs 8:17	ASV
Ephesians 6:24	ASV
Jeremiah 29:13	NIV
Psalm 46:1	NIV
Acts 2:21	NIV
John 8:31	CEV
I John 4:18	NKJV
Job 42: 1-6	NLT
Galatians 2:16	NLT

CHAPTER 2	CHAPTER 2
2 Timothy 1:13	TLB
1 Peter 2:2	NIV
2 Corinthians 1: 8-9	NIV
Matthew 11:28	TLB
John 15:5	NKJV
Genesis 2: 1-3	NLT
Isaiah 58:13	NIV
Matthew 12:8	NLT
1 Timothy 4:8	TLB
Jeremiah 31:3	NIV
Philippians 4: 6-7	NLT
Philippians 4:7	NLT
Jeremiah 29:13	NIV

CHAPTER 3	CHAPTER 3
Proverbs 18:10	NIV
Job 24:14	TLB
John 10:27	NLT
Matthew 16:18	MSG
Luke 22: 31-33	TLB
Psalm 119:114	NIV
Luke 15: 28-32	NIV
Matthew 6: 9-13	NKJV
John 8:44	NLT
2 Kings 5: 9-15	NLT
Jeremiah 18: 1-10	NIV
Isaiah 41:10	NIV
Romans 5:8	NIV
Mark 5: 35-43	NLT

Hebrews 6:19	MSG
2 Kings 4: 2-6	NLT
Hebrew 3:15	NIV
Matthew 16: 16-17	NLT
Matthew 6:6	NLT
Matthew 27:40	NLT
2 Corinthians 13:5	NLT
2 Peter 1:3	TLB

PART 2	PART 2
CHAPTER 4	**CHAPTER 4**
John 3:5	TLB
Nehemiah 4: 1-7	NLT
Nehemiah 6: 15-16	NLT

CHAPTER 5	CHAPTER 5
Proverbs 1: 1-7	NLT
Ecclesiastes 12:13	KJV
Jeremiah 32: 39-41	NLT
Ephesians 1:11	MSG
Psalm 119:96	NIV
John 10:10	AMP
Jeremiah 32:41	NLT
Matthew 5: 14-16	MSG
Matthew 5:13	TLB
1 Corinthians 13: 2-3	TLB

Chapter 6	CHAPTER 6
Romans 5:4	NLT
Genesis 18: 10-15	TLB
Hebrews 11:11	TLB
Jeremiah 29:11	TLB
1 Corinthians 15:33	NIV
1 John 3:2	MSG
2 Corinthians 5:17	NKJV
Romans 12:2	AMP
Titus 2:7	NKJV
Proverbs 3: 5-6	NIV
Matthew 7:21	TLB
2 Timothy 1:7	TLB
Galatians 5:22	NLT

CHAPTER 7	CHAPTER 7
John 3:27	TLB
Philippians 1:9	TLB
Philippians 4:13	TLB
Matthew 5: 29-30	NKJV
Romans 8: 35-39	NLT
John 4: 34-38	NKJV
Exodus 3: 10-15	TLB
Luke 9: 23-24	TLB
Matthew 25: 28-29	NLT
Ecclesiastes 3	NLT

PART 3	PART 3
CHAPTER 8	**CHAPTER 8**
John 13: 34-35	MSG
Matthew 5:16	TLB
1 Corinthians 12: 22-26	NLT
Galatians 5: 22-23	NLT
Romans 12:5	NIV
Matthew 5: 43-48	NIV
Acts 2: 44-46	TLB
Mark 3: 33-35	NKJV
John 13: 34-35	TLB
1 John 4:8	NKJV
John 17: 22-23	NKJV
1 Chronicles 29: 3-5	TLB
2 Corinthians 9:6	AMP
Luke 16: 8-12	NIV
Acts 2: 42-47	NLT
2 Corinthians 9: 5-15	TLB

CHAPTER 9	CHAPTER 9
Hebrews 9:15	NLT
Judges 21:6	NIV
Judges 21:25	NIV
Proverbs 13:22	NLT
Acts 20:32	TLB
1 Chronicles 29:19	TLB
2 Kings 2:9	TLB
Proverbs 13:4	NIV
Psalm 1:2	TLB
Matthew 22: 37-40	NLT
Psalm 22:30	NLT
John 9:4	NLT
John 17	NIV

APPENDIX II

References & Resource Materials

Nicky Gumbel

Try Alpha – alpha.org

Alpha is a series of interactive sessions that freely explore the basics of the Christian faith

Bill Johnson

Hosting the Presence: Unveiling Heaven's Agenda, Paperback

Publisher: Destiny Image Publishers (27 Mar. 2013)

ISBN-10: 0768441293

ISBN-13: 978-0768441291

Andrew Wommack

Financial Stewardship, Paperback

Publisher: Harrison House (May 2012)

ISBN-10: 1606834002

ISBN-13: 978-1606834008

FOOTPRINTS OF GRACE

S. Michael Houdmann

Got Questions? Bible Questions Answered—Answers to the Questions People Are Really Asking, eBook

Publisher: WestBow Press, 2014

ISBN: 1490832734, 9781490832739

Rick Warren

Purpose Driven Life, Paperback

Publisher: Zondervan; New edition (2 Nov. 2002)

ISBN-10: 0310210747,

ISBN-13: 978-0310210740

APPENDIX III

Hymn Must I Go, And Empty Handed

Lyrics supplied by Hymnal.net

1   "Must I go, and empty-handed,"
     Thus my dear Redeemer meet?
     Not one day of service give Him,
     Lay no trophy at His feet?
     "Must I go, and empty-handed?"
     Must I meet my Saviour so?
     Not one soul with which to greet Him:
     Must I empty-handed go?

2   Not at death I shrink nor falter,
     For my Saviour saves me now;
     But to meet Him empty-handed,
     Thought of that now clouds my brow.

3   O the years in sinning wasted;
Could I but recall them now,
I would give them to my Saviour,
To His will I'd gladly bow.

4   O ye saints, arouse, be earnest,
Up and work while yet 'tis day;
Ere the night of death o'ertake thee,
Strive for souls while still you may.

Words: Charles Luther (1847 – 1924)

Music: George Coles Stebbins (1846-1945)

APPENDIX IV

Death Bed Letter

"I reached the pinnacle of success in the business world. In others' eyes, my life is an epitome of success. However, aside from work, I have little joy. In the end, wealth is only a fact of life that I am accustomed to...

At this moment, lying on the sick bed and recalling my whole life, I realize that all the recognition and wealth that I took so much pride in, have paled and become meaningless in the face of impending death. In the darkness, I look at the green lights from the life supporting machines and hear the humming mechanical sounds, I can feel the breath of the god of death drawing closer...

Now I know, when we have accumulated sufficient wealth to last our lifetime, we should pursue other matters that are unrelated to wealth...

Should be something that is more important:
Perhaps relationships, perhaps art, perhaps a dream from

younger days ...

Non-stop pursuing of wealth will only turn a person into a twisted being, just like me.

God gave us the senses to let us feel the love in everyone's heart, not the illusions brought about by wealth. The wealth I have won in my life I cannot bring with me.

What I can bring is only the memories precipitated by love. That's the true riches which will follow you, accompany you, giving you strength and light to go on.

Love can travel a thousand miles. Life has no limit. Go where you want to go. Reach the height you want to reach. It is all in your heart and in your hands.

What is the most expensive bed in the world? – the "Sick bed"

You can employ someone to drive the car for you, make money for you but you cannot have someone to bear the sickness for you.

Material things lost can be found. But there is one thing that can never be found when it is lost – "Life". When a person goes into the operating room, he will realize that there is one book that he is yet to finish reading – the "Book of Healthy Life".

APPENDIX

Whichever stage in life we are at right now, with time, we will face the day when the curtain comes down.

Treasure love for your family, love for your spouse, love for your friends...

Treat yourself well.

Cherish others